OVERPOWERED!

OVERPOWERED!

THE SCIENCE AND SHOWBIZ OF HYPNOSIS

Christopher Green

THE BRITISH LIBRARY

CONTENTS

INTRODUCTION

The whole atmosphere of educated society is filled with this subject. In every company the conversation turns upon it, and it infects the air around us. Some are sceptical; some are frightened; some despise the whole thing, and assert it to be all imposture; some play with it as an amusement; some seek to the clairvoyant or to the dead to remove their anxieties and gratify their curiosity; some receive and yield themselves to the influence of the mesmeriser or to the guidance of the spirits professed to be invoked. Some regard it as a mere subject of philosophical inquiry, and assert that they can explain it all on scientific principles.

FROM *WHAT IS MESMERISM? AND WHAT ITS CONCOMITANTS CLAIRVOYANCE AND NECROMANCY?* FRANCIS SITWELL, 1862

The wonderful and hyperbolic hypnotist Walford Bodie. He captioned this as 'Hypnotising Wild Beasts in the Zoo', in his modestly titled *The Bodie Book* in 1905. Can beasts in a zoo really be described as wild? Discuss.

Yeah, alright! So Francis Sitwell was a little giddy in the opening paragraph of his book about mesmerism. It's a bit over the top, but to my mind there's nothing wrong with a degree of exaggeration. (I always, always exaggerate). I would hesitate to make such huge claims about hypnosis today, but there's no doubt that the practice is firmly lodged in our collective consciousness – it beguiles and intrigues us. The range of its fascination – from fear, to the occult, to science, to healing – hasn't changed much since 1862.

I love hypnosis because I don't know of any other subject that is at once so erudite and yet so trashy. It's about brain imaging in laboratories ... and it's about wearing flashy suits under stage lights. It's peer-reviewed and recommended by the World Health Organization, yet it can't shake off its low-rent, disreputable image. The two branches of the subject – the science and the showbiz – are usually kept separate these days, but this hasn't always been the case. These twin identities have merged and separated at points throughout history,

But enough of the facts and figures, I hear you saying ... what about ME?

leaving most of us today with a confusion of half-remembered half-truths about what hypnosis really is.

I also don't know of another subject that provokes so many questions: 'Can I be hypnotised?' 'Will I lose control?' 'Can it stop me eating cake?' The smoke-and-mirrors of the showbiz is infused into the therapeutic practice. Sometimes this is useful, most often it is not. Practitioners of either branch of the discipline tend to dislike their counterparts, yet borrow heftily from them. Mystery is at the heart of hypnosis – it's another of the reasons I love it. And yet at its core, hypnosis is bewilderingly – even, perhaps, disappointingly – simple.

This book is my very personal power-jog through the peaks, valleys, suburban sprawl and brownfield sites of the strange land of hypnosis. It will introduce you to some of the big personalities through the years, and – brace yourself – there will be extraordinary moustaches. It will give you some science, some history, lots of pictures of old-time folks doing it. But enough of the facts and figures, I hear you saying ... what about ME? Can hypnotism help stop my annoying habits? Can I do it to myself? Can I do it on the cheap? Will it

enable me to transcend reality? Do I need a moustache?

I'll give you a brief overview of hypnosis from before it was even called that, up to the present day. It's an astonishingly complex story, but this is not the place to go into the big arguments, competing theories and rival factions. There are lots of other books that go into that kind of detail. My focus is on how the science and the showbiz started off together, before splitting acrimoniously – and despite getting together for the occasional reconciliatory shag in the intervening years, they have stayed resolutely apart. And though I'd love to give you a neat factual history, like a biography of some dry historical personage, hypnosis resists all attempts to pin it down. It's a slippery beast. The last two hundred years have really been the story of lots of people – mainly men – trying to keep hold of the slipperiness. This is demonstrated by the recurring theme of people right at the heart of the business suddenly turning around and declaring that it isn't real. For example Hippolyte Bernheim (1840–1919) was a leading figure in the main branch of French hypnotism in the late nineteenth century. After years spent establishing himself as an august elder statesmen of the practice, he abruptly popped up and proclaimed '*Il n'y a pas d'hypnotisme*' ('There is no such thing as hypnotism'), which caused more than a bit of fuss. Slippery indeed.

This inherent uncertainty at the heart of the practice is why I'm not going to try to pin everything down – and besides, I'm naturally much more interested in the attendant personalities: the people who made money from it, the people who made it an art form. When you're attempting to describe something as elusive as the operation of the human consciousness, you simply can't deal exclusively in hard facts. Therefore consider this book a celebration of the doomed exercise of attempting to theorise on the ultimately elusive fairy dust of hypnosis.

I am often amazed by the capacity of human beings to make things complicated. Many people have a lot invested in making straightforward things appear highly specialised. You could see this book as a guide to the various ways in which experts in the field have succeeded in making the intricacies of hypnosis as inaccessible as possible to everyone else. There have been great fights about different approaches to the same technique, and different schools of thought. I'll introduce you to some of these factions; I'm interested in them, but not invested in any of them. Hypnosis is a very personal thing – it's about what makes sense to you. I do wonder, however, if sometimes we simply need sophisticated-seeming strategies to shock us into being healed.

This book is called *Overpowered* because I am fascinated by the delight human beings derive from the idea of being taken over. Being conscious may be beneficial, but it's also hard work. Relentless. And so much of our culture seems to be about relinquishing this responsibility for ourselves. Some people are desperate to become famous so they can be looked after by teams of managers and stylists, submitting to the tender ministrations of celebrity. We are still horrified and yet fascinated by the idea of Adolf Hitler, who seemed to have an entire country in his power. I'm not saying that watching television is like being controlled by Hitler, but to some extent don't we sit in front of a big flat box every day just so we can turn down our own consciousness for a while? We like being overpowered, although we know we shouldn't. It's no wonder, then, that hypnosis fascinates us – though with a dose of fear and a dash of mockery to guard against it.

The two branches of hypnosis that we have today are both riddled with clichés. Hypnotherapy is often dismissed as hippy, self-help nonsense with more than whiff of essential oils about it. Stage hypnosis, meanwhile, is the preserve of sad blokes on tawdry stages in Crimplene suits. However, I promise you that hypnosis is so much richer than that.

I'm going to take you through enough of the history to show how we've arrived at these two distinct, and equally misunderstood, manifestations of the same discipline. I'm also going to tell you why I became interested, because that might help show that hypnosis can be both highly diverting and also extremely useful in helping us make sense of the great mystery of being alive.

Ultimately, hypnosis encourages all of us to examine our relationship with our own consciousness. This is less diverting, and much more hard work, but in the long run much more profound, than men in cheap suits getting people to pretend to be chickens. At its best, hypnosis demands that we look at the story we tell ourselves about ourselves. It shines a light on that self-narrative, and firmly yet gently encourages us to retell this story. And the possibilities arising from that are endless.

For myself, I have distilled all this phenomenal potential down to one construction:

'How would it be if ... ?'
How would it be if you were as powerful as you know yourself to be?
How would it be if you were content/philanthropic/a leader/a healer/a frivolous show-off?
How would it be if you were healed/were free/weren't afraid of dogs, or spiders, or buttons, or death? Or life?
How would that be?

Everything human beings do is habit.
All habits can change.
Hypnosis is a fast track to changing habits.

And that's the nutshell.
Want a bit more detail?
Hold on to your fob watch, we're off ...

The Peculiar Gaze of the Hypnotized.

THE HISTORY

All the way through human history you can find practices that look a lot like what we call hypnosis. And I wonder if, not that far in the future, it will be called something else but still look pretty much the same.

Stretching back into prehistory you can find rituals designed to induce something that appears to be trance. (Whether it is a trance or not is a question that has dominated much of the recent history of hypnosis – but hold on a bit, we've got that to come.) We are familiar with the idea from primitive societies that various ceremonies, shamans, dancing and chanting, or combinations of these, can produce an altered state that may induce physical or spiritual healing. In ancient Egypt there were sleep temples in which you could be cured through chanting, suggestion and the induction of something like a trance. There were similar places in ancient Greece and the Middle East, and they sound rather brilliant. Should we bring them back? I'm all for it. But to be clear, I'm for hospitals too.

However, the real story of what ended up being hypnosis starts with one man, much later. You might be surprised to discover that there was an actual person who gave his name to a state of pliant being, and in so doing became a household name: Franz Anton Mesmer. He made big breakthroughs in treatments in the 1770s

Opposite: 'Animal magnetism – The Operator putting his Patient into a crisis'. Hard though it is to ignore the magnetism coming from his hands, look at the electricity passing from his eyes to hers. I feel a bit swoony myself.

Left: The French wilfully misunderstanding the notion of 'animal' magnetism to comic effect (with a disconcerting whiff of bestiality).

LE MAGNÉTISME ANIMAL

Importante Découverte par Mr. Mesmer, Docteur en Medecine, de la Faculté de Vienne en Autriche.

Il est prodigieux la quantité des Malades gueris par cette methode qui consiste dans l'application d'un fluide ou agent que ce medecin dirige tantôt avec un de ses doigts, tantôt avec une Baguette de Fer qu'un autre dirige à son gré sur ceux qui recourent à lui. Il se sert aussi d'un Bacquet auquel sont attachez des Cordes que les malades nouent autour deux, et des fers recourbez qu'ils approchent du creux de l'Estomach, ou du foye, ou de la Ratte, et en general de la partie du corps dans laquelle ils souffrent. Les malades sur tout les Femmes éprouvent des Convulsions ou crise qui amenent leur guerison, Nombres de personne attaquée de Paralisie, d'hidropisie, de la Goute, du Scorbut, de Surdité accidentel, ont été gueris. Mr. Mesmer recommande la Gaieté et ce qui peut l'inspirer.

and 1780s. (This chapter is fast-moving, isn't it? We're out of the realm of prehistoric people in penis sheaths dancing round fires, and into the realm of fellas in wigs. Keep up.)

The history of modern hypnosis is a parade of different men: doctors, scientists and entertainers who all inched the practice forward while engaging in lots of high-octane arguments and gossipy catfights with their fellow practitioners. I'm not going to go through all of these people for you – the various plot twists and turns are as complex as series one to five of Dallas in the 1980s – but let's sum it up by saying that hypnosis looks as it does now because of all of them (and JR survived). Rather, I'm going to tell you the stories of the most famous and influential of them. I'd say that if one image could sum this story up, it would be a high-status man, slightly winging it, leaning over a hysterical woman and using experimental, mysterious

Opposite: Mr Mesmer's Tub. At the height of his fame Mesmer created a fantastic pseudo-scientific baquet or 'tub' which had metal rods sticking out of the edge. Patients would touch the afflicted parts of their bodies against the rods in slightly orgiastic gatherings involving music and high hysteria. It's like a foam party without the foam.

Below: Puysegur's tree, from *Hypnotism* by Foveau de Courmelles (1891). It's a complex story but basically the Marquis de Puysegur 'magnetized' a tree and things got a bit hectic.

> ... if one image could sum this story up, it would be a high-status man, slightly winging it, leaning over a hysterical woman and using experimental, mysterious forces to calm her down.

forces to calm her down. I would love to write an examination of the subject from a feminist perspective, in fact, but then there wouldn't be any room for the lovely pictures. Just keep this agenda in mind.

Suffice to say that the moment Mesmer's story really kicked off was when, as a young doctor in Vienna, he decided to treat a hysterical woman with multi-systemic failures by getting her to swallow a lead solution then making strange passes over her with magnets. (Obviously!) Slightly surprisingly, she slowly got better. Mesmer didn't think it was just the magnets, though – he thought it was down to an invisible fluid passing out of a sick patient under the control of a healer by a process called animal magnetism. He became a sensation, and the practice of mesmerism was born. To say that his actual treatment sounds bonkers to us today is an understatement, but as the ubiquity of the word that bears his name shows, he certainly started everyone thinking. Mesmer didn't enjoy a straightforward career from this point; he had many failures and kept disappearing from the public view, and his last years were spent as a bird-mesmerising recluse ... but his legacy was immense. His most

ANIMAL MAGNETISM;
SIR RHUBARB PILL MESMERISING THE BRITISH LION.

Opposite: A menu of different magnetic practices in 1893 including some of our favourites – Mesmer's Tub, Puysegur's Tree, and Abbé Faria simply shouting at a woman. Illustration from *Les Mystères de la Science* by Guillaume Louis Figuier, 1893.

Left: Abbé Faria stonily demonstrating the powerful subjugation of a weak-willed woman.

Right: That's better! Much more reassuring than the image on page 13 is a good old-fashioned British wilful misunderstanding of the notion of 'animal' magnetism. 'Punch's Pencillings – no.VI – Animal Magnetism; Sir Rhubarb Pill mesmerising the British Lion', 1841.

prominent follower was Armand-Marie-Jacques de Chastenet, Marquis de Puységur, who has – perhaps not surprisingly – not become a household name in the same way. However, he moved Mesmer's thinking on by inducing 'magnetic somnambulism', which looks a lot like what most people today think of as hypnosis. In fact it is really Puységur, not Mesmer, whose work has been the most influential, and first gave the practice its twin forums of therapy room and stage, but history isn't very fair or logical about these things. (Perhaps nineteenth-century people were embarrassed that they couldn't spell his name?) But it was at this point that the world of hypnotism was first divided into two gangs: 'fluidists', who still believed in Mesmer's magnetic fluid, and 'animists' who viewed it as something psychological.

The next fella to progress this therapy was the enigmatic Catholic priest Abbé Faria, who demonstrated animal magnetism in Paris in the early nineteenth century. He was given to commanding an entire audience to 'SLEEP!' – a bold theatrical move. He was an animist who thought that mesmerist's suggestions were the primary influence on subjects, and that they experienced what he called 'lucid sleep'. After him came a plethora of men with various theories leaning over various weak-willed women, and impressionable men giving demonstrations of mesmerism. It was to one of these demonstrations that a Scottish doctor called James Braid went in 1841. He was intrigued by what he saw, but he made a few changes before trying it himself, and he also came up with a new name. He called it hypnosis …

More of him in a while, though. I think it's time for some personal history. My name is Christopher and I'm a hypnotherapist.

MY STORY

PART ONE

It was New Year's Day. A good day for a new start, surely. We were staying in our friend's spare room, and I woke early and listened to a hypnosis MP3 I'd downloaded from the internet. This was my first experience of hypnosis. The closest I'd come before was at university when most of my friends went to see a stage hypnotist, but instead I went out on a date. If I'd not been in pursuit of sex I might have started this profound journey of self-realisation two decades earlier. The sad thing is, if I had my time over, I'd probably do the same again.

I was driven to the MP3 by my bird phobia. Let's look at that language. My bird phobia. I could have said 'I didn't like birds much', but no. I *owned* it, as evidenced by the word 'my'. And it was definitely a phobia. That gave it real status. Now, though, I would say that I had simply got into the habit of being afraid. As I pointed out in the introduction, everything human beings do is habit, and all habits can be changed. Fear is just a particularly powerful one.

Either way, it really got in the way of life. My husband learned never to suggest eating outside because of EVIL seagulls. Never eating anything outside is a huge concession to make to fear – and to ask the person you love to make alongside

you. I was once standing outside Sydney Opera House with two important producers. A bird swooped near, and I hit the deck. It was embarrassing to say the least. But essential.

I had asked my therapist to help me with this fear. She would say (can you imagine an intense Italian accent for this, please?) 'I wonder what the bird represents? Is it your parents? Is it me? Is it your nihilism?' She said she thought it was my super-ego that was trapped and unable to fly. I said I just wanted to go on a picnic without crying. What I'm telling you is that she didn't help.

I don't know where I got the idea to download the self-hypnosis MP3.

Desperation probably inspired it. It was probably also very cheap, and would have seemed like a much better deal than paying to actually see someone. I didn't think hypnosis was much more than a joke, but I was starting to get bored of avoiding places with lots of birds – I knew something had to be done. So, while I was sceptical, and while the rest of the household slept, I listened. I remember having a lot of negative thoughts in my head, about how stupid the whole thing was. 'How naff is this music? How embarrassing is this voiceover? How pointless will this entire exercise turn out to be?' But before the hypnosis started, the voice said 'there are thousands of people who used to be afraid of birds walking down every street', and I thought 'oh, I'll become one of them, then'.

I had never role-modelled being OK before. Before that I used to aspire to count myself among the interestingly screwed-up. Think about it: our culture celebrates people who elevate dysfunction to an art form. We are encouraged to be like them, and I was rather good at that. But think of a positive role model? I didn't even know who that could be. Jesus? Oprah?

Quite simply, the hypnotic session strengthened my resolve to not be afraid of birds. It melted away and dissolved the fear that I would feel so much panic the world wouldn't be big enough for my pain. I could feel it working. I could feel myself letting go of the panic that I had made a habit. The mysterious aspect of the hypnotic process allowed me to see beyond the pain that is involved in letting go of pain. And it was so easy – I became someone who used to be afraid of birds. It really was that simple. Later that day I walked into a throng of pigeons on the canal towpath and they got out of my way. They didn't hate me. They weren't trying to ruin my day. They were smelly and a little bit disgusting and they flapped in a way I didn't really like, but I didn't panic. And that's still the same today.

Because I'm the kind of person who overthinks things, my imagination started

The mysterious aspect of the hypnotic process allowed me to see beyond the pain that is involved in letting go of pain.

to run away with itself. What else about myself could I change so easily and efficiently?

So, I went on a one-day course to learn the basics of hypnosis. And being me, I took it further, and within three years was fully qualified as a cognitive behavioural hypnotherapist. Straightforward story, huh? But in that time everything about my life changed. The first section of the hypnotherapy course came just after my husband was diagnosed with cancer, the second was just before he was given a terminal diagnosis, and the third fell a year after I was widowed. Over that time period I came off antidepressants, stopped drinking and taking drugs, stopped being depressed, started running … and started being, if not always loving to myself, at least civil. I started to uncover the vast capacity that had always been in me to be happy. Hypnosis led to mindfulness, and then to daily meditation. Death and grief are powerful motivators – for destruction or liberation. Hypnosis was simply the technique I used to make sure that the devastation would set me free. And I used it. And I still use it.

So while I might joke and be flippant about all this stuff, I really do think it's powerful – because it's not about what somebody can do to you, it's about what you can do for yourself. It's about self-care, self-respect, and changing the stories you tell yourself about yourself. If that makes your head spin, good. Because it should. If it makes you panic, then I'd suggest you are listening to the fear that change brings up, and I'd advise you to push through the pain to what lies on the other side. Or, alternatively, keep flicking through the book and look at some of the moustaches. It's up to you.

But for now, let's get back to the big history. Hypnosis is about to be born. Gather round like the animals in the stable …

It's not about what somebody can do to you, it's about what you can do for yourself. It's about self-care, self-respect, and changing the stories you tell yourself about yourself.

THE HISTORY

THE TRIUMPH OF HYPNOSIS

In 1841 James Braid went to a public performance in Manchester by a demonstrator of animal magnetism called Charles Lafontaine. Braid was impressed by the effects, but he believed that the same results could be brought about without contact with the subject.

His theory, which he put into practice very quickly on the same public stage two weeks later, was that the results occurred not because of animal magnetism, or telepathy, or any other voodoo, but because of ordinary processes of the body and brain, such as concentrated attention on the part of the subject and suggestion from the operator. He got a bit fixated on the importance of eye fixation, and underestimated the importance of the power of suggestion, but he undoubtedly created a shift in thinking. He called his development neurohypnology. The sad thing is that when you look at his original papers you can see that he was most particular about his new coinage from a linguistic point of view, but history has not been so careful. It comes from the Greek – the favourite language of erudite medical types – meaning 'a discourse on nervous sleep'. He knew it wasn't real sleep; he was using the term as a metaphor, and

he called it 'nervous sleep' to make this clear. But people are still confused about this distinction to this day. Most people think that sleep, and unconsciousness, are prerequisites for the hypnosis process to take place. (Metaphors can be dangerous, kids! Tigers they are. Well not tigers in the sense … oh Hell – see what I mean?) Braid did later suggest the term 'hypnotised' instead of 'mesmerised', but the word 'hypnosis' wasn't generally used until many years later.

Anyway, Braid had caused what can only be called a conniption in the world of mesmerism. Slowly, slowly hypnosis took over from mesmerism – with slowly being very much the operative word. Mesmerism was still being talked about and practised very freely in the late-nineteenth century, and it is still an incredibly common word now. Which is strange when you consider that it is generally agreed that it was discredited in 1841.

James Braid – physician, surgeon, mesmeric revolutionary and, incidentally, the man who gives the lie to the standard advice in men's fashion magazines that sideburns automatically give you cheekbones.

Extase somnambulique.

In the salons of Paris the craze was for somnambulist parties. For all its elegance it does have a lot in common with hen parties as the fellas watch the girls dance. I particularly dig the piano player who must be giving it some mean trills.

At that point mesmerism had spread its wings far, and especially to America. There was a long history of Europe in general and Britain in particular shipping the more idiosyncratic ideas of the time over to the United States. Religion, spirituality in general, politics … all found a new home. America was almost like a Petri dish where extreme notions could flourish outside of the host body. Flourish, develop, breed and diversify. And exciting things happen when these developments return to their place of origin. Much of what is interesting about the history of the twentieth century, it seems to me, is about that process, and the same is abundantly true in the specific history of this subject. Many of the somewhat kooky ways in which mesmerism developed in the US in the

nineteenth century came to inform how hypnosis was regarded and represented in the twentieth century, both there and in Europe — from movies and the stage, to spirituality and the consulting room.

Mesmerism, even from the early days, seems to have been regarded differently in the US. Nathaniel Hawthorne, an American novelist and short story writer, wrote two novels in the 1850s, *The House of the Seven Gables* and *The Blithedale Romance*, which feature the supernatural, witchcraft and the sinister power of mesmerism. They are about the exercise of dark powers over the weak and vulnerable. They are properly weird. This was a strange, spooky world, this mesmerism business, which of course was mixed up with pseudo-science. For example, it was

> **The adventures of mesmerism in late nineteenth-century America would make a great TV mini-series.**

intimately involved with phrenology – the belief that certain parts of the head related to particular organs in the body. Magnetic fluid was directed to the relevant bit of the head in order to cure the afflicted organ. Empirical, peer-reviewed data is hard to come by for phrenomagnetism. But it later morphed into electrobiology, harnessing the power of the new invisible wonder, electricity.

Electrobiologists are most interesting to me because they loved a stage demonstration. There was nothing particularly new in that, as all the mesmerists, hypnotists and other characters liked to stand on stage – but because of the introduction of the electrical element, the behaviours that the electrobiologists liked to induce in their subjects formed the basis of what later became the stage hypnotism show. The main aspect of this was that the subjects could be made to perform out of character, and anyone who has seen a formerly shy hypnotised man pretending to be Freddie Mercury on stage will know that this is a staple of a modern hypnosis show. They also liked to provoke involuntary actions, the inability to feel pain,

and catalepsy (a trancelike state involving the loss of voluntary movement).

The adventures of mesmerism in late-nineteenth-century America would make a great TV mini-series. If HBO jumped on this, a great plot strand would have to be the strange spiritual mash-up between spiritualism, Swedenborgianism and animal magnetism. Swedenborg was a spiritual leader who died in 1772 whose New Church was undergoing a revival. Animal magnetism was what Mesmer called the inivisible natural force exerted by animals. They came together in the figure of Andrew Jackson Davis. After all, to mesmerise someone using the tenets of a seventeenth-century Swedish philosopher in the name of God is a fantastic cultural feat.

There were similar influences on other less-than-conventional religions, such as Christian Science and New Thought, and Phineas Parkhurst Quimby is a little bit of a favourite of mine from around this time. He is known as 'the father of self-help psychology', and he combined many practices, eventually leaving mesmerism behind. He found he didn't need it; he could heal without it.

Andrew Jackson Davis. Known as the John the Baptist of spiritualism and the Ploughkeepsie Seer, he rocks for many reasons but mainly because he based his practices on Swedenborg despite claiming never to have read his works.

Helping people to heal using whatever works seems a pretty modern concept. This is relevant, because obscure and bonkers though all this sounds, it did directly influence how we think of hypnosis today. It meant that the subject gradually belonged less to the world of the high-status doctor or aristocrat – as was the case in Europe – and more to ordinary people. To the ordinary preachers and teachers. Self-appointed visionaries sprang up throughout the second half of the nineteenth century, and they weren't interested in people's health, but in working on their mind and their spirit. If the Old World was your crusty old neighbourhood GP equivalent, these New World guys were Oprah.

Back in Europe, hypnotism steadily asserted itself. In lecture halls, music halls and town halls hypnotic demonstrations were taking place. Some were 'conventional'; some were intertwined with spiritualism, a touch of the occult or even some of the American notions such as electrobiology. Many practitioners advertised themselves as delivering a hybrid range of techniques, such as 'mesmerist and electrophrenologist'. But hypnotism, more or less as defined by Braid, which relied primarily on the power of suggestion, was most definitely in the ascendancy.

(Hang on, we're nipping over to France at this point, because many consider the period from 1880 to 1890 as being the first golden age of hypnosis. Just how golden it was is doubtful, as most of the interest seems to have been the big scrap that was going on between rival Gallic hypnotists. It's all about a wrestle between the Salpêtrière Women's Asylum ... and Nancy. And if you think this sounds like a bizarre spin-off of Charles Dickens' *Oliver Twist* involving a reincarnated plucky heroine hopelessly outnumbered by some old-time loonies, you'd be wrong.)

Jean-Martin Charcot was the Chief of Medicine at the Salpêtrière Women's Asylum in Paris in the 1860s. He loved hypnosis, and he practised on the poor women in his charge. Some of them were really good hypnotic subjects. Why? Well,

If the Old World was your crusty neighbourhood doctor, these New World guys were Oprah.

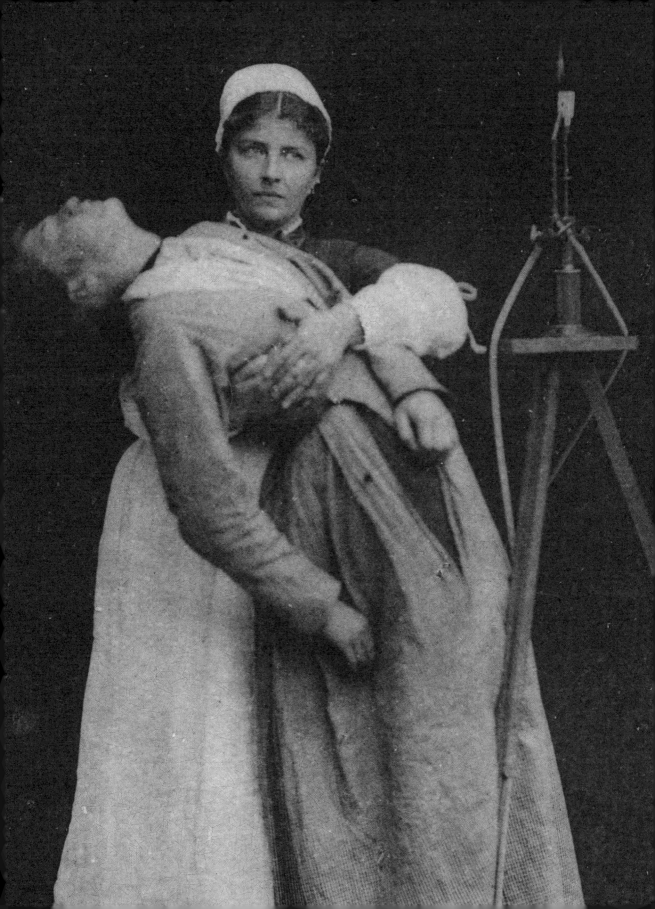

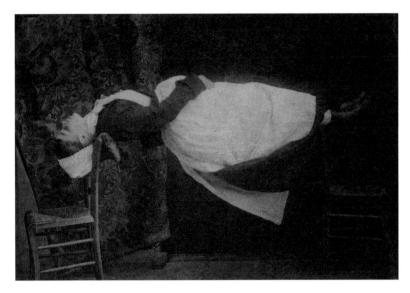

it's hard to know for certain, but I suspect being locked up in an asylum didn't offer many opportunities for play – and this did. Also they were probably allowed crazy luxuries like food afterwards, so I'm not sure how scientific it all was, and a Swedish doctor at the time felt the same. He described watching Charcot getting a woman to eat charcoal after she was told it was chocolate, rocking a top hat having been told it was a baby, and barking on all fours on the floor like a dog. (It's up there with Abu Ghraib as one of the all-time entertainment hotspots of history.) However, Charcot was formulating serious scientific theories. He defined 'grande hypnotisme', which basically said that hypnosis was a manifestation of hysteria. This pretty extreme view was surely going to be challenged by someone – and Ambroise-Auguste Liébault, from Nancy in north-eastern France, stepped up to do just that. He was a colleague of Hippolyte Bernheim. (Surely with a great name like that, you'll remember him? He was the one

who caused a later conniption by stating that there was no such thing as hypnosis.) Well Bernheim and Liébault went head to head in a rap battle with Charcot and the grande hypnotisme school, involving lots of complicated arguments about the nature of trance, hysteria and what they had done to each other's moms, etc. Eventually this led to Charcot's defeat, and the birth of a 'hypnotherapeutic' movement.

Now I'm going to go back to Britain and rewind to the 1840s. Something else was happening just at the time Braid made the giant leap forward into hypnosis from mesmerism. Lots of things were happening of course, but I'm not noble enough of mind to know about politics or social movements. I'm talking about what was happening round the backs of pubs. Not filthy goings-on involving guardsmen and the minor members of the aristocracy, though I'm willing to watch that movie if you're willing to make it. I'm talking about the birth of the British Music Hall. It's my other area of obsession and so

This series of images of women from Salpêtrière are very beautiful and disturbing. The women are objects first, patients second and people somewhere after that. The image of the hypnotic plank tells you all you need to know. This book is full of different versions of the plank. But this is science, in a medical facility with patients being held against their will. It's a long way from a Vegas Supper Show.

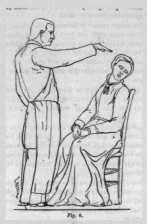

The standard 'fella hypnotising a woman' image with the addition of two notable elements – an apron and a snake. The latter is all very Garden of Eden, and the former is a worry.

it's interesting that the 1840s is the time when both hypnotism and Music Hall came into being. I think what happened then is the start of the split in hypnotism that has continued to widen right up until the present day – I'm talking about the split between science and showbiz. Remember that the history of mesmerism and hypnotism, like that of many other medical and psychological disciplines, is the story of public demonstrations of new developments. These were open meetings; for members of the professions, mainly doctors, but also for any gawkers who fancied a bit of entertainment. We just don't have this platform today. If these had carried on, there would be a regular sensationalist medical TV show in which the latest practices were beamed into our

sitting rooms. For sure, there are worthy documentaries, and gory operations, but certainly not high-status medical thinkers effectively saying 'I'm making this up as I go along, but I reckon it should work… let's try it on little Daisy here.' Culturally we decided it was a good idea to keep the flashy showbiz out in the open, and to largely hide the serious thinkers away inside big buildings, from which they pop out from time to time when they've really thought something through and know that it works. It seems a shame but, put like that, it's probably the best system.

The birth of Music Hall signalled a sea change in entertainment. There was an enormous circuit of venues: not just music halls; some more erudite, like town halls; some even more low-rent, like the penny gaffs. But many of my favourite hypnotists – whom we will meet in the coming pages and whose vitality is still evident from the ephemera housed in The British Library – took advantage of all of these. A generation earlier they would have needed some scientific or medical credentials, but at this point they could generally just make them up. It's all the context required. They could put together an act that was

---

Culturally we decided it was a good idea to keep the flashy showbiz out in the open, and to largely hide the serious thinkers away inside big buildings, from which they pop out from time to time when they've really thought something through and know that it works.

---

still largely a demonstration in form, with all the hallmarks that the old mesmerists had made part of the vocabulary – such as the high-status operator, the low-status subject, the catalepsy, the miraculous results. In fact this is still the terrain of the stage act of hypnotism today. (Most people who go for hypnotherapy have to be warned that this is not what they are going to experience while being cured for their inability to remain calm in the presence of a chocolate fountain.) But the pressures associated with the performance context, the audience who were coming for shock and spectacle as much as serious science, the need to get bums on seats, the pressure to have better posters than your rivals – all these factors gradually led to the division between science and showbiz. Many of the people I am drawn to from the archives are attractive to me – I think – because they seemed to want to cross that divide. They wanted to help people as well as entertain them. Like me, I feel, they seem to occupy a middle ground between science and showbiz, which is self-help. But the strict demands of entertainment meant that unlike the out-and-out healers in America, they stuck to being

entertainers first and slightly shamefaced secret shamans second. It's all very British, isn't it?

So now, somewhere around the end of the nineteenth century, mesmerism has more or less gone, though its presence lingers on. Therapeutic hypnosis – as outlined primarily by the Nancy School in France – has been established, and there are lots of people merrily hypnotising away for entertainment. It would seem very unlikely that this flourishing art would decline in the first half of the twentieth century, right? (Guess what! You can find out in the next history chapter, entitled 'The Decline of Hypnosis in the First Half of the Twentieth Century' …)

But first, before we leave the glory days behind completely, lets look in more detail at some gems from the nineteenth-century stages and lecture halls.

MYSTERIOUS SCIENCE

NINETEENTH-CENTURY STAGES, SCIENCE AND THE SUPERNATURAL

The mind exercises a powerful influence over the body. From the beginning of time, the sorcerer, the interpreter of dreams, the fortune-teller, the charlatan, the quack, the wild medicine-man, the educated physician, the mesmerist, and the hypnotist have made use of the client's imagination to help them in their work. They have all recognized the potency and availability of that force.

The nineteenth century was the period when the mind came into its own. After the rationalism of the Enlightenment, the powers of imagination, dreams, science, mystery and the occult exploded in the popular consciousness. Mesmerism and hypnosis were an important part of this.

There is obviously something going on with these practices – anyone can see the results – but *what* exactly was hard for them old-time folks to work out. We shouldn't blame them, either – because we are still not entirely sure ourselves. It's all to do with the power of imagination excited by the power of suggestion, but back then this was layered with many confusing distractions. I love those distractions. The sinister, the showbiz, the shameless scams … I love them.

One of the first times I became aware of hypnotism as a child was while reading the autobiography of Mark Twain. Of course, before reading this, I had been exposed to endless confused cultural notions of 'the hypnotist' and 'being hypnotised'. Children pick it up from nowhere in particular, after all, though I do remember one character – the Hypno-Clown from *Scooby-Doo*. It's hardly surprising that I do remember him, because he is super-scary: you've got all the clichés right there. The hypnotic induction through use of the fob watch, the evil staring eyes, the desire to control in the name of pure evil. He might have a different big nose but he is basically Svengali, the absolute embodiment of the evil hypnotist from *Trilby* by Du Maurier, of whom more later.

Kennedy was an American showman; this is from the 1890s. The figures climbing out of the mouth of the moon and gambolling all around it seem to suggest Bruegel rather than a night of hilarity. Probably heavier on the screams than the laughter.

Back to Mark Twain. He tells a memorable story from his childhood, in which the travelling mesmerist comes to town. He plays along, and becomes a stooge for the mesmerist, acting as though he is totally under the influence and even allowing the mesmerist to put pins in him. He became the star of his small town. Years later he tried to tell everyone the truth – that he was just playing along – but nobody believed him. Because nobody *wanted* to believe him. However, the burden of the lie lay heavy on Twain: 'The glory which is built upon a lie soon becomes a most unpleasant encumbrance.' If you don't know this passage it's well worth hunting out. It's entertaining, and funny, and the moral of the boy who cried wolf is memorable – but also Twain does put his finger on a central slipperiness at the heart of hypnosis, which is why I find it so fascinating. Twain becomes the perfect hypnotic subject for reasons of his own. He is young and unformed and wants the attention. But that doesn't make him an out-and-out faker. Hypnosis is nothing more than taking suggestions, and letting those suggestions play over you. Does motivation really matter? Of course that makes the practice vulnerable to fakers, and tricksters, but that doesn't mean that it hasn't 'worked'. That slipperiness, that lack of scientific credibility, makes it hard for us in our empirical age but again this comes back to its roots in the nineteenth century, when the overlap between science, pseudo-science, entertainment and what we would now call self-help, made for a delightful grey area.

One of the things I find most engaging is that, though there have now been over two centuries of debate, strops, tantrums and academic studies about all aspects of hypnosis, the fundamental character of a demonstration hasn't changed. The through-line between a mesmeric demonstration in the 1840s and a hypnosis demonstration today is clear to see. One of my most beloved discoveries is a detailed description of Annie De Montford's (see Women and Hypnosis) stage routine. It runs to several pages, but it really is a delight. The narrative is exactly the same as it would be today, with some cultural variants – getting volunteers up on stage, whittling them down to the best performers, giving simple suggestions that become increasingly complex. For example, she got them to pick flowers and be afraid of wasps, believe that their coats were on fire, find pigeons in their coats, pretend to be a troupe of minstrels, and re-enact a battle with some Frenchmen. It's not that far from getting elderly ladies to be Lady Gaga or burly blokes to dance like ballerinas.

The vagaries they performed as her bidding were of a most ludicrous character, and created much merriment amongst the audience.
The Star, 16 September 1880

Mesmerism could take place anywhere – from a huge public demonstration to a few people gathered in a parlour. These 'séances' weren't the preserve of any social class – it was a great leveller. Some people were fascinated by it as a life-changing experience that challenged the hegemonic power of religion, state and science; others liked it for a nice day out.

This obscure advertisement is very revealing. It was apparently not seen as strange that at a big public gala a mesmerist, in this case Professor Smalley, would present a mesmeric demonstration. The notion of singing, reciting and dancing

in a mesmeric state sounds remarkably like a modern stage hypnosis show. People might now draw the line at impersonating the Ethiopian Serenaders – a blackface minstrel troupe from the 1840s, although I'm sure that sort of caper still went on in some shows in the 1970s. And a mesmeric tea party sounds so innocent; so removed from the supernatural connotations that often accompanied mesmerism. But then this wholesome, teetotal aspect was a huge part of popular mesmerism in this period. It shows how complex and multi-

GRAND BAND of HOPE DEMONSTRATION, and JUVENILE GALA.

The Committee of the Bradford BAND of HOPE UNION have pleasure in announcing that they have made arrangements for

A GRAND GALA,
to be held in
PEEL PARK, BRADFORD,

On SATURDAY AFTERNOON, August 2, 1862, for the joint benefit of the Band of Hope Union and the Peel Park funds.

A JUVENILE CHOIR of 1,000 VOICES

will occupy the Great Orchestra, and at intervals sing a selection of Popular Melodies, with Band Accompaniments, under the able superintendence of Mr. Amos Firth.

Books of Words, printed for the occasion, may be had in the Park.

Arrangements have also been made with Professor Smalley, the celebrated Mesmerist, for a grand

MESMERIC DEMONSTRATION,

to commence at Six o'clock with a Mesmeric Tea Party; singing, reciting, and dancing whilst in a mesmeric state, and a personification of the "Ethiopian Serenaders." To conclude with a "Teetotal Discussion."

The following BANDS will also be in attendance during the Gala, and play a selection of the most popular music of the day :—Marriner's Keighley Prize Band, Heaton Brass Band, and Allerton Juvenile Drum and Fife Band.

Beautiful and Variegated BALLOONS will ascend at intervals, and during the evening, Sports, Amusements, &c., will be introduced, so that all assembled may have an ample opportunity afforded them for enjoying themselves.

Gates open at Two o'clock.

The Committee desire that those Bands of Hope who can make it convenient, will walk to the Park in procession from their various meeting-rooms.

A REFRESHMENT BOOTH will be provided.

ADMISSION.—Ladies and Gentlemen, 6d. ; Working Classes, 3d. ; Children under 14, 2d.

Tickets will be issued at a reduced rate to adult members of the Band of Hope, Sunday Schools, and Temperance Societies, at 2d. each ; Children, members of the same, 1d. each.

No tickets at the reduced rate will be sold after Friday, August 1st.

The members of the Bands of Hope will be supplied with tickets at their Meeting-rooms.

Sunday Schools and Temperance Societies can be supplied on application to the Secretaries, ALFRED LIVERSEDGE, 33, Bright Street, Lister Hills; and THOMAS COX, 10, St. Jude's Square, Manningham Lane.

Arrangements are pending with the various Railway Companies in Bradford to run SPECIAL TRAINS, at reduced fares, from the surrounding districts. For Fares, &c., see the Company's bills.

Bradford *Observer*, 24 July 1862. Mesmerism took place anywhere – from huge public demonstrations to a few people in a parlour. These séances weren't the preserve of any social class – it was a great leveller. Some people were fascinated by it as a life-changing experience that challenged the hegemonic power of religion, state and science, and some liked it for a nice day out.

This handy chart looks like something that might have come free with the Sunday papers for you to stick on the fridge. After all, doesn't everyone need an informative ready reckoner to the basics of phrenology and animal magnetism for when the kids ask tricky questions?

'Phrenological and Mesmeric Chart' by Dr J. S. Butterworth, c. 1850s.

faceted the discipline was, and a long way from Svengali, or the evil hypnotists of the twentieth-century cinema screen.

This handy chart looks like something that might have come free with the Sunday papers for you to stick on the fridge. After all, doesn't everyone need an informative ready reckoner to the basics of phrenology and animal magnetism for when the kids ask tricky questions? Phrenology, which bases everything on a study of the skull, was all the rage (as you'll remember) in the early part of the nineteenth century. It was a natural ally of mesmerism and animal magnetism. And it is also a classic pseudo-science, with all the appearance of rational thought intercut with knee-jerk reactionary clap-trap. (Even the Royal Family had their children's heads examined.) And all these diagrams of brains and heads look very satisfying and like they should mean something … even if we are not sure what exactly. I think it's important to bear this in mind when looking at brain scans, which is our current obsession. If it's come out of a MRI scanner it must be important, we think. Yet I couldn't decode what was happening on a brain scan without it being interpreted for

me by an expert, so we are as reliant as ever we were on the scientist.

This chart demonstrates perfectly the fray that James Braid entered when he outlined his theories of hypnosis in the 1850s. I would sum it up from looking at this chart by saying that there appear to be a lot of big heads with not much in them – but that's a layman's opinion.

Eloquent Ephemera

There are many ways to look at popular hypnosis in the second half of the nineteenth century. I'm not going to take the high-status, received-wisdom, academic approach by looking at the big stars of the period. I think the best way to capture the vibrancy, the moral complexity and the rich textures of the subject in this period is through the pamphlets and advice books written by the contemporary practitioners. In most cases 'pamphlet' is definitely the right word; 'book' would be over-stating it. But the writing of pamphlets was a noble tradition, and it reached its zenith in this period. Pamphlets were the blogs of their day; a cheap, easy form of communication, from someone with information to impart or simply an axe to grind.

THE PHRENOLOGICAL AND MESMERIC CHART.

By J. S. BUTTERWORTH, Hulme, Manchester.—Lecturer on Mesmerism and Teacher of Practical Phrenology, &c., &c.

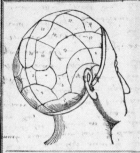

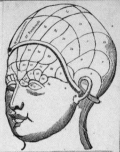

HYDROCEPHALIC

Lectures on Natural History, &c., 10s. each, for Mechanics' Institutions. Seven hundred Testimonials, speaking highly of the Lectures, may be seen by Persons engaging him.

Mr. J. Butterworth begs to intimate that his terms for marking down an account the respective sizes of the Cerebral Organs, is One Shilling; and for the same, with a written analysis of character, Three shillings.

Families waited upon at their own residences; attendance at his Place, Bedford Street, Great Jackson Street, Hulme, Manchester.

Phrenology may teach us the character and disposition of those to whom our destinies are to be united; it may prevent more cruel disappointments in parents, for it will show the capacities of their children, so that they may be apt to make trades or professions. Do we want to know the true character of a servant, clerk, or shopman, we need only to study the unerring laws of nature, as taught by Phrenology.

	£	s.	d.
Four Lectures on Phrenology and Mesmerism,			
Two 1s. sea ons do.	3	0	0
Two 1s. do. do.	1	15	0
For Institutions, each Lecture	0	15	0

CLASSIFICATION OF THE ORGANS

Order 1.—Feelings and Propensities.

1. AMATIVENESS.
2. PHILOPROGENITIVENESS.
3. INHABITIVENESS.
4. ADHESIVENESS.
5. COMBATIVENESS.
6. DESTRUCTIVENESS.
7. SECRETIVENESS.
8. ACQUISITIVENESS.
9. CONSTRUCTIVENESS.

Genus 2.—Sentiments Common to Man.

10. SELF-ESTEEM.
11. LOVE OF APPROBATION.
12. CAUTIOUSNESS.

10. BENEVOLENCE.
14. VENERATION.
15. FIRMNESS.
16. CONSCIENTIOUSNESS.
17. HOPE.
18. WONDER.
19. IDEALITY.
20. WIT.
21. IMITATION.

22. INDIVIDUALITY.
23. FORM.
24. SIZE.
25. WEIGHT.
26. COLOUR.

27. LOCALITY.
28. NUMBER.
29. ORDER.
30. EVENTUALITY.

TEMPERAMENTS.

LYMPHATIC.
SANGUINE.
FIBROUS.
NERVOUS.

ANIMAL MAGNETISM.

The science of Animal Magnetism will in due time prove its claims to the attention of mankind. This science was well known to the ancient philosophers of Egypt, Arabia, and Greece.

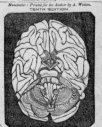

TENTH EDITION.

May be had from all Booksellers, or of A. Heywood, Oldham Street, Manchester.

I found many of these hypnotists' pamphlets in the British Library collections. They are often little more than ephemera … but then I love ephemera. Often what is inadvertently left behind speaks so eloquently of a time that is lost. A performer makes work that exists only fleetingly, and it is the posters, the flyers and the merchandise that will remain – and that's a peculiar thought. The glories of a live performance, a hypnotic demonstration that might have electrified an audience and really changed lives, can only be glimpsed through the booklet that was for sale on a stall afterwards, probably cheaply produced, designed to take advantage of the rush of excitement and a giddy loosening of thrift that an audience collectively experiences after a great show when they are still a little bit in love with you. Designed to give the performer a means to buy supper and the train fare home. (I'm talking about myself here, but I'm pretty sure I'm not far off the mark.)

All of these books play a teasing game. They promise to reveal everything about the practice, but in reality they give away little. There are diagrams, pictures, instructions, expansive prose on the potential of the practice to effect social and personal change – but ultimately they can't capture what it is about hypnosis that keeps it alive. You can't blame a slim pamphlet for that. Nobody has been able to capture it. (It's slippery, you see.) And yes – I am aware that my description of these pamphlets could probably apply to this book. You can see that I'm following in a noble of tradition of smoke and mirrors.

The perfect example of this genre is 'Dr. Vints Secrets of Hypnotism Revealed'. If you google Dr Vint, you'll only get me writing about him. I've invented historical scams for dramatic purposes that have way more in the way of support material than Dr Vint: he only seems to exist in this tiny book. Obviously he has a fantastic moustache, but we don't know much else. Written in 1891, even the title page warms and slightly breaks my heart. It

---

All of these books play a teasing game. They promise to reveal everything about the practice, but in reality they give away little.

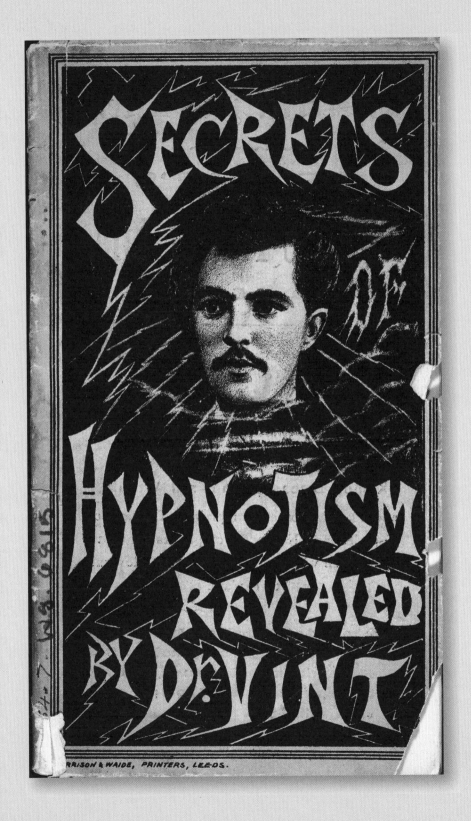

SECRETS OF HYPNOTISM REVEALED BY Dr VINT

RRISON & WAIDE, PRINTERS, LEEDS.

I love the irony that this reproduction of Dr Vint's little booklet is infinitely more lavish and glossy in this reproduction than in the shoddy original.

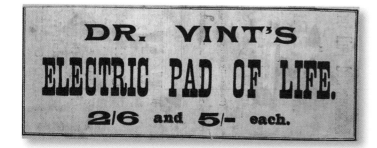

The mysterious Electric Pad of Life. Admit it – you would click through to purchase if you could….

advertises itself as being for anyone who wishes 'to alleviate the suffering of their fellow creatures'.

Dr Vint writes that 'I have greatly enlarged this edition'. This edition consists of 47 pages, so the previous edition must have been pithy to say the least. Handling this artefact today is a lovely feeling. This tiny collection of printed pages is so fragile to have survived unexpectedly all these years. Its cheap print quality and what appear to be home-produced illustrations make no claim to biblio-immortality in the way that a leather-bound volume does. The fact that it requires a stiff-backed envelope to live in at the library makes me love it more. But then I like the low-status. Once, in a British Library reading room, somebody with an Important Academic Tome open in front of her asked me,

sniffily, why I didn't just go to a second-hand bookshop for 'that sort of thing' as I feverishly made notes on the *Tammy Wynette Southern Cookbook*. What a snob! (I take comfort in having the moral high ground and better cornbread.)

Dr Vint believes in empowering his reader; I am presuming he also gave demonstrations. Conventional wisdom dictates that he should have upheld the idea that he was the one with the power. But he makes it more powerful by giving it away. (This attitude informed my Singing Hypnotist character, who starts off as the one with all the power, and gradually transfers it to the audience.) Dr Vint writes 'Most persons possess the power of curing others … Health is transferable as well as disease.' That must have been an incredible thought to a late-nineteenth-century reader, terrified by the diseases all around them in the big cities that the majority of the population now lived in.

I love Dr Vint's railing against ill-informed opinion. In fact I'd love to sit with him on a sofa watching a random selection of contemporary TV. I'm sure he would be shouting at it. 'It is surprising how many persons in the world have no

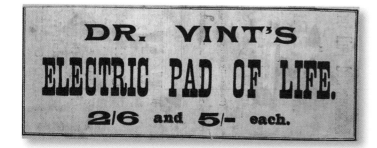

DR. VINT'S
ELECTRIC PAD OF LIFE.
2/6 and 5/- each.

force of character: are only big children, holding silly opinions on various subject of which they know nothing.' He loves his subject passionately, and concludes: 'One thing is certain, the medical fraternity are beginning to realise the fact that mesmerism will soon become one of the most important and pleasing sciences. Scoffers will eventually take a back seat, scepticism evaporate into thin air and from the chaos of the war between doubt and truth, the latter will boldly stand forth conqueror in the name of "Mesmerism and Hypnotism".' Claims like this can be found on virtually every clinical hypnotherapist's website, although without the pleasing Victorian hyperbole. The war against the 'scoffers' is always just about to be won.

But without any doubt, the most intriguing thing Dr Vint has to offer is on the back of his pamphlet.

This is presumably absolutely nothing to do with hypnosis. There is no clue whatsoever as to what the 'Electric Pad of Life' is. But doesn't it sound like something you would want – even *need*? I have thought about it at length, and decided that the five-inch version is the better value. Did Apple steal all their ideas from him? Is this an early iPad with two models? I can only imagine this was another product range that Dr Vint sold after shows, because there is no order address. The use of the word 'electric' here brings together the new science and the new healing. If electricity was involved in something with the whiff of hypnosis then it was deemed to be a Good Thing. This idea is manifest in the naive art on Dr Vint's front cover. It's all about thought waves, hypnotic control and even animal magnetism – rendered to evoke electrical currents.

All these 'how-to' guides – hypnotic handbooks and mesmeric manuals – use the terms 'mesmerism' and 'hypnosis' almost interchangeably. As James Coates says in his book from 1897 (the title alone demonstrates what I'm saying), *Human Magnetism or How To Hypnotise: A Practical Handbook for Students of Mesmerism*, 'practically, hypnotism is mesmerism. The phenomena being observed being similar, change of name cannot alter them.' James Braid and many others may have disagreed, but we are talking popular psychology here after all, and it was a long time after Braid. I say the terms were used almost

Right: Coates using the good old-fashioned James Braid method of inducing hypnosis.

Far right: Coates using the fancy Nancy method of induction.

Opposite: James Coates titled this image 'Testing Susceptibility'. I reckon that the participant seems to be not very susceptible judging from his stiff body.

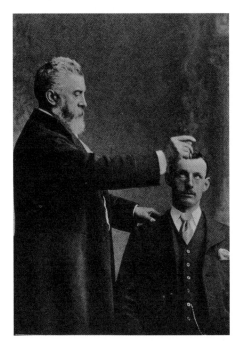

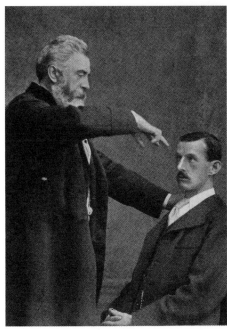

interchangeably because there was then – as now – an important distinction between the two that the popular elision between the words can't quite get at. Mesmerism or magnetism – animal or human – carries a strong whiff of the supernatural. In the second half of the nineteenth century a lot of scientists wanted to cleanse the subject of that whiff, and the term 'hypnosis' achieved that. The sinister reputation that mesmerism conjured up in the collective imagination was just not there with hypnosis; but then again, so much of the richness and complexity of the subject was bound up in the notion of mesmerism that even the most scientific writer couldn't resist referring to it from time to time.

It's all very imprecise and messy. And by the mid-1890s hypnosis was also lost to the mainstream thanks to the raging success of George du Maurier's novel *Trilby*, featuring the fictional hypnotist Svengali. It

was sinister as well as scientific. You can almost sense the frustration felt by writers of the time in trying to make their subject seem entirely rational, even clinical, and yet not being able to resist the call of the mysterious. For example, many of them refer not to sessions or treatments but 'hypnotic séances', even though this word was already tainted by connection with the supernatural.

All of these tensions are apparent in another of my favourite manuals. This pamphlet from 1886 makes Dr Vint's seem like a weighty tome: 'The Secret of Mesmerism. With Full Instructions How To Mesmerise.' This has 15 pages, and it is a big claim for such a slender volume. I would personally say that its 'full instructions' aren't as full as you might wish, but it is priced at 'One Penny' and is therefore excellent value. Its author is anonymous, but is described as 'A

Physician'. Its tone is much more sober than Dr Vint's, and the aesthetic more austere. The tension between rationality and the supernatural elements is felt on every page. Most fascinating of all, it carries two warnings. The first is a warning to the practitioner, and I am guessing that buried deep in this warning might be the reason the author decided to remain anonymous. He warns the mesmeriser: 'Having once succeeded in placing a subject fairly in the mesmeric state, a form of infatuation is only too ready to seize upon the operator, and may lead to a neglect of the ordinary duties and avocations of life and unfit him for the position of a useful citizen.' (Wow. The power went to his head! He has a full-on addiction to putting people under.) But it gets worse than that, and he has a greater warning for anyone about to hypnotised: '… still greater evils lie in wait for the unfortunate subject. Bewildered and fascinated by the strangeness of this new sensation, he willingly and eagerly rushes to a repetition of the influence. Soon his mental vigour is withered, his self respect is gone, and his strength of purpose reduced to that of a child or an imbecile.'

This incipient moral panic – that social disintegration is just around the corner – might seem farcical to us now, but it is a very human trait. New practices, and especially new technologies, still freak us out. I love descriptions from the 1950s of the moral decline that would be visited on our country if working-class women were allowed to go out and play bingo. They seem quaint to us now. But isn't our current obsession with the neurological change in teenagers' brains brought about by addiction to pornography the same thing? 'Bewildered and fascinated by the strangeness of this new sensation, he willingly and eagerly rushes to a repetition of the influence.' Call it neuro-plasticity, moral panic or doomsday. It was ever thus.

How to Hypnotise (Including the Whole Art of Mesmerism Embracing All the Latest Discoveries of the Schools of Germany and France) by John Barter, Teacher of Shorthand, is another favourite. I would love any manual that contained the line 'in order to stop this screaming …'. It, again, is very revealing about how the subject was regarded in the period. Published in 1890, it makes an even bigger claim than 'The Secret of Mesmerism', promising

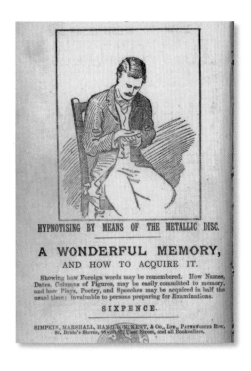

HYPNOTISING BY MEANS OF THE METALLIC DISC.

A WONDERFUL MEMORY,
AND HOW TO ACQUIRE IT.

Showing how Foreign words may be remembered. How Names, Dates, Columns of Figures, may be easily committed to memory, and how Plays, Poetry, and Speeches may be acquired in half the usual time; invaluable to persons preparing for Examinations.

SIXPENCE.

SIMPKIN, MARSHALL, HAMILTON, KENT, & Co., LTD., PATERNOSTER ROW, St. Bride's Stores, 56 and 57 Fleet Street, and all Booksellers.

John Barter is inducing this Prince Albert look-a-like into hypnosis using his patented metallic disc. He also takes the opportunity to plug another of his books.

to impart how to hypnotise, including the whole art of mesmerism and all the wisdom of the new German and French schools. I'm not sure how Charcot and his European colleagues would have felt about all of their discoveries being summed up as an afterthought in a book that is only 32 pages in total. We have looked at a book written by a stage hypnotist, and a physician, and now this one written by Barter, who proudly asserts himself as a teacher of shorthand. To our eyes this is a little like me promoting myself as a performer because I have a certificate in how to use Excel spreadsheets, but in actual fact it reveals much about the importance placed on new technologies. Shorthand and the typewriter were part of the bright new world of clear thinking a million miles away from clerks scratching away in a Dickensian office. Barter declares himself Modern, and he is also the proud author of Barter's *Guide to Good Handwriting*, and *How to Write and Address a Letter*. His book, while in no way delivering on the grandiose claims of the title, is bold and clear in its approach, but with a heavy reliance on gadgets, such as the metallic disc in the illustration.

I suspect Barter of making stuff up to some extent in this list of qualifications of a good mesmerist:

'1. the most suitable age is between 23 and 50. (females become as good operators as men)
 2. it is well he should have a muscular and commanding appearance: though not essential.
 3. he should have confidence in his own powers because confidence begets confidence'

However, he was on the money with the list of persons who make the best subjects. Remember, it's all about the exercise of power:

'1. young females
 2. females generally
 3. the debilitated and weak but not the restless
 4. young men

> **'Let the operator now place the tip of his forefinger on the Organ of Imitation … and his sensitives will immediately begin to imitate the screaming of the parrot.'**

5. men generally who are in a passive state of mind – for this reason soldiers are easy to mesmerise.'

Earlier I mentioned the mash-up of mesmerism and phrenology – the study of different areas and shapes of the head. Well, John Barter and also D. Younger, who we will read about soon, were very big on something called phrenomanipulation. It's a very simple and pleasing notion – if you touch the right spot on the head, a specific character trait or behaviour will be provoked. For example touching the area which is called 'Tune, will excite to sing, or play on an imaginary instrument'. Or if you touch 'the Organ of Veneration' it will 'produce a display of religious feelings with, at times, very eloquent prayers, delivered with much fervour'.

Barter's book has surely the best instruction in any how-to manual ever: 'Let the operator now place the tip of his forefinger on the Organ of Imitation, situated on either side of Benevolence and his sensitives will immediately begin to imitate the screaming of the parrot, or of any animal suggested in a marvelously

accurate manner to the great amusement of the audience.'

As to Barter's instructions on how to mesmerise water … I think he should have stuck to shorthand.

In summary, I think I love these booklets so much because they seem democratic in nature. They sell the idea that anyone can pick up the essentials and become an influential person, like the mesmerist Annie De Montford, who went from being a mill worker to 'her mind governs the world'. They are DIY manuals, *Dummies' Guides* of their time. If they were being created now they would be a series of YouTube videos.

The American advert overleaf sums up that spirit. Just like a YouTube clip, the book is offered for free. (Presumably there must have been some upselling going on later.) I've never heard of Professor Harraden, but apparently he was 'the greatest hypnotist of the century'. He unwittingly uses what I think is the defining description of hypnosis, which sums up all the tensions I have been talking about with regard to the supernatural vs. the rational, mesmerism vs. hypnosis, etc. He

Prof. L. A. Harraden's

COMPLETE MAIL COURSE
OF TWENTY ILLUSTRATED LESSONS IN
HYPNOTISM

COPYRIGHTED 1899
BY
L. A. HARRADEN
JACKSON
MICH

calls it a 'mysterious Science'. That's it, and I use that phrase a lot to describe what I'm doing with my show. The capital S on 'science' gives it weight, which is somehow neutered and yet also beautifully enhanced by the word 'mysterious'. And let's face it, who wouldn't want to 'reform a misguided friend'? (NB: You can't do this with hypnosis – repeat after me: 'Everything I've seen in films and TV is wrong – I can't make someone do what they don't want to do.'). Also, he is representing the great moustaches posse … and look at those hypnotic eyes! (I hope for his sake it was a hyperbolic engraving and not a dodgy thyroid.)

The big daddy – and I use this phrase advisedly – of nineteenth-century hypnosis handbooks was D. Younger. His book from the late 1880s was definitely *not* a pamphlet. It's a heavyweight, like its author. It is called *The Magnetic and Botanic Family Physician*, and would grace any middle-class family's bookshelf. Younger seems to have identified as a mesmerist, but from the illustrations it all looks very much like hypnosis, and some of it very modern. Mind you, whatever language he used I'm sure he was persuasive. He seems to have been the embodiment (and what

a body!) of patrician Victorian manhood. (He also seems to have specialised in working with little fellas – or perhaps that's just to make the techniques more impressive.)

While much of this looks like classic hypnosis to the untrained eye – high-status operator exerting influence on a lower-status subject – in fact, as he says, this is mesmerism or electrobiology. There is a lot of emphasis on not touching the subject, to allow the magnetism to flow. The text reveals little about suggestion – and remember, that is all hypnosis really is – and more about the biological currents. There's quite a bit of phrenomanipulation. He is seen 'exciting the Organ of Veneration', which is a little disappointing because it simply means touching the top of the head. The illustration of him 'breathing down the fingers into the ear for deafness' is pure quackery. My favourite piece of advice from the text is when Younger suggests to a patient that he goes to live in Australia because the climate is better there. He reports that this treatment is a complete success, and the subject doesn't want to come back. Couldn't afford to or couldn't face the journey are

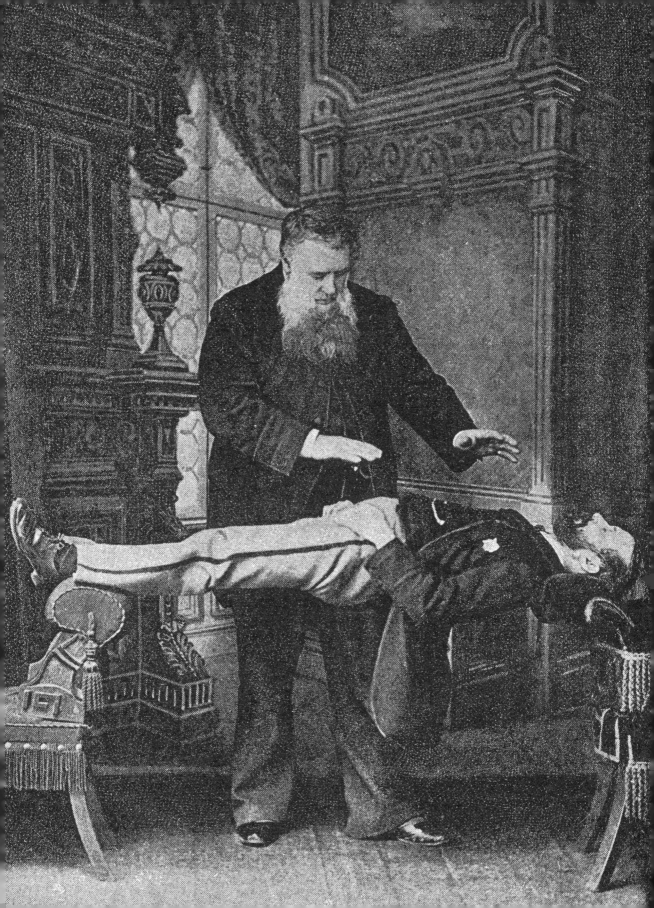

also possibilities ... but I'm being a cynic.

Younger starts his book with two epigrams. Neither of them is massively inspirational:

The first care of the true Physician should be not to injure his Patient. Dr Dickson

There is no difference whatever between Hypnotism and Mesmerism. D. Younger

That's right – he quotes himself in an epigram at the start of his own book; not only that, he quotes himself making quite a dull point. But he is at least democratic in his approach to the subject, even gung-ho: 'The command of Jesus to "heal the sick" was not restricted to his disciples; and if considered perfectly safe in the hands of simple fishermen then, surely the uncultured of the present day may be trusted.' Oh OK – you go first, then.

Showing that he is bizarrely obsessed with Australia and that he isn't, despite his first epigram, overly worried about the sensitivities of his patients, he gives us this gem: 'A very interesting drawing room or evening party entertainment can be practiced by stringing together a series of incidents such as might be expected to occur on a voyage to Australia.' Every detail of said voyage – from the tedious (eating cabbage leaves for their first meal on board) to the dramatic (the ship almost sinking) – is recounted. It sounds like the patient might be traumatised by all of this. Still, it's a lot more interesting than a lot of stage hypnotism shows I've seen.

The undoubted highlights of this book, however, are the many adverts at the back of it for Younger's huge range of Alofas Safe Herbal Remedies, to cure everything from ringworm, to piles, to cholera (with Safe Cholera Syrup). I find it very moving

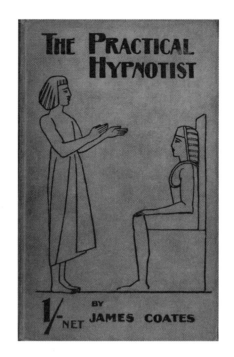

to read about what people obviously suffered from; we are all still vulnerable to human frailties in this way. I fancy some of the general Alofas powder, which cures loss of vitality, brain fog, weakness, rickets and much more. (Order me a 2s 9d packet.) 'The daily use of this powder cheats the grave of its premature victims.' (Make that a 4s 6d packet!)

So this book is strictly a pre-hypnotic historical oddity, and only interesting to those who like hypnotism, or people who like to see big men exerting control over little ones.

At this point, it's time for a word about the cataleptic state. This does look very modern, doesn't it? We have seen it thousands of times: it's a hypnotic classic. And as Younger demonstrates, it goes all the way back to mesmeric demonstrations. A few of my favourite examples are in this book. Be very clear, though, that this is a stunt that has nothing to do with hypnosis. When used in conjunction with hypnosis, the subject will worry about it less and it will be more effective, but it is actually a carefully stage-managed illusion. The chairs are arranged so that from the front it looks as if one is under the neck and the

other under the ankles, but in reality they are providing a lot more support than that. So it's simply a balancing act, and you should never see it on stage in a hypnosis show. And yes, it's dangerous for the spine, but more than that – it's just not hypnosis.

It's interesting to compare Younger's book with James Coates' book *The Practical Hypnotist. Concise suggestions in the art and practice of suggestion; applied to the cure of disease, the correction of habits, development of willpower, and self-culture in 1905*. Here there's still the patrician operator, but the tone is much less flowery: we are definitely talking hypnosis now. Although the final image shows that magnetic healing is still on the cards, it's now listed as 'one method of treatment'. Coates is writing, he says, because 'Whilst a few are familiar with the literature of the subject, the bulk of the British public obtains its ideas of hypnotism from paragraphs in the daily press and

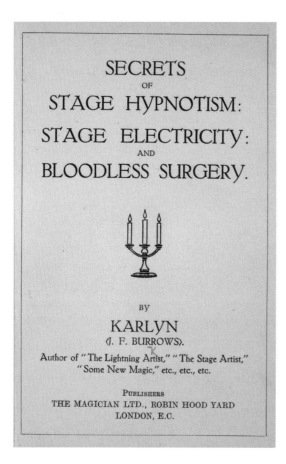

Imitation being the sincerest form of flattery, I know that Karlyn would be delighted I nicked his front cover for my own.

from public entertainments, and those are frequently misleading.' Good luck with that one, James. Nothing has changed in the century since.

The cover of Coates' book shows an Egyptian hypnotist working on a pharaoh. This is either totally inspired – because it is very different from any other iconography used in a book of this type, and it conjures up images of mysterious intrigue – or the unnamed illustrator wasn't great at drawing people from the front but excelled at profiles. Either way, it rocks.

Coates calls his book a 'brochure', which I like very much indeed – though it is, in reality, just a pamphlet. He also

calls hypnotism 'suggestive therapeutics', which is an excellent name. It would still work today for a rebranding of hypnotism. (Except that we are still so weird about sex that the word 'suggestive' now simply means 'saucy', doesn't it? So suggestive therapeutics could be imagined entirely differently – possibly a disappointment to someone being charged £80 a session.)

Coates is very interested in the relationship between thought and body, which feels very modern. He likes the phrase 'what he believed himself to be, he was'. And this is an interesting notion: 'If it was as fashionable to talk about health as people do of disease there would be more health.'

Following that line of thought, he is very down on negative discussion of hereditary illness – 'You know his father died of—?' I suspect he would therefore disapprove of a lot of modern medical practice, where every possibility is named and tested for in the full knowledge of the patient. Does this bring on more illness? I'm sure it does. It's all in the power of suggestion – that is to say, it is incredibly powerful.

So Coates' *The Practical Hypnotist* is definitely that – practical and no-nonsense. It is all about willpower and 'self-culture' (a phrase that seems very ahead of its time), and the image of the subject experiencing lethargy is surely one of the many that has seeped into our collective consciousness. This is precisely what nobody wants. A rest and some relaxation is a nice notion, but being zombified like this is horrific. This has more to do with the power of the hypnotist as a reverse Frankenstein – taking the essential life force away from somebody – than any idea of healing.

This leads me nicely to the final hypnosis handbook. Written in the brave new world of 1912, it focuses firmly on the stage. You might recognise the cover of Karlyn's book. The stage hypnotist Karlyn

was in fact J.F. Burrows, and he wins on many fronts. (Mainly for having the best moustache it is possible to have.) However, it is his obsession with stage electricity that makes this book brilliant. There are detailed diagrams of how to build lethal-sounding machines to deliver mild electric shocks to participants on stage. He tells you how to light a volunteer's cigarette using thousands of volts of electricity. And how could you not want to deliver an electric kiss? Could you live without knowing how to set fire to a volunteer's handkerchief by electricity conducted by a sword?

Burrows/Karlyn gives advice on everything from poster design ('Electrical and hypnotic effects lend themselves readily to striking pictorial announcements') to stage demeanour ('[stand] there gazing at the audience with the air of a king looking upon his subjects'), but it is his revelations about how he conducts his stage hypnotism that are more shocking than the thousands of volts of electricity he used. Burrows states that the hypnosis he uses is 'pretence and not reality'. 'The subjects experimented upon are employed by the performer and are instructed before coming upon the stage

Karlyn the epitome of the showman from his admirable root lift, to the sheer girth of his collar, from the swagger of that stare to the thrusting bravado of the best moustache in the business.

to do as they are told.' They draw regular weekly salaries from him. They are … 'in effect, actors in a little comedy company'.

He is a detailed practitioner who knew what he was doing. He gives away enough secrets to make this book a fascinating, even shocking, read – but not in enough detail for anyone to actually copy his act. In fact they would have had more respect for his stagecraft (if they could see their way clear to overlooking the audience plants and general charlatanism). That's what he is counting on, at least. 'The public understand just how much of the act is genuine work, and just how much is a mere matter of showmanship.' Skilful slight of hand there – bloodless surgery was

an emotive subject, and here it was laid out for anyone to have a go at, from the preparation before the show with 'cripples of all ages and degrees of infirmity'. It still is an emotive subject – have a look on YouTube if you don't believe me (but ideally not after you've eaten). All in all this is a practical guide that wasn't to be beaten – until Ormond McGill's masterly *New Encyclopedia of Stage Hypnotism* in the 1990s.

Let's end this section, though, by giving power to the people. Which is exactly what the miraculously named Xenophon LaMotte Sage did. (I'm seriously considering having three more children so each can receive just one of these splendid monikers.) Perhaps inspired by the words of D. Younger about the 'uncultured of today being trusted' to hypnotise like Jesus trusted his disciples, Xenophon wrote and sold a correspondence course in how to hypnotise, going out via the mail all over America.

It consists of 36 lessons on typed sheets. Its production values are basic. The British Library has just acquired a copy, and I got to look at these fragile sheets before they went into the archive. If you are one of those people who opens a consumer

---

Lesson 24 teaches you:
'how to hypnotise a large number at once,
how to hypnotise a man in a crowd,
how to extract a tooth under hypnotic influence,
how to relieve pain,
how to hypnotise by telephone, by mail, by
telegraphy and at a distance.'
Yes – all of that in one lesson!

---

durable and likes to just turn it on, this isn't the course for you. It is very bossy and full of bold-type warnings and cautions to READ THE INSTRUCTIONS VERY CAREFULLY. It helpfully points out '[to] be sure that you thoroughly understand just what to do before attempting to hypnotise anyone'. Most thrillingly I imagine, if you were receiving this in your humble home, there are various exhortations to 'Keep these instructions strictly private'. There's an extra sheet with special instructions on post-hypnotic suggestion, and the legend 'Keep private' very large at the top. This makes it all seem much more powerful and exciting that I'm afraid it is in reality. Great marketing though!

I enjoyed reading the lessons, though was slightly worried by the uneven pacing of the course. The first few are as basic as you might expect, then there is a huge leap in the required skill-set in the teens, and then Lesson 24 teaches you:

'how to hypnotise a large number at once, how to hypnotise a man in a crowd, how to extract a tooth under hypnotic influence,
how to relieve pain,

how to hypnotise by telephone, by mail, by telegraphy and at a distance.'

Yes – all of that in one lesson! And all in three pages (with pictures). I actually know how to do some of these things – and even I wouldn't be confident following these instructions. It does make clear that it's not possible to hypnotise from a distance, but then gives some instructions for how to do so anyway on the off-chance it might work. It's patchy, too. The entirety of Lesson 32 is only six lines long, simply on 'use of the hands'. I might have put that earlier – before tooth extraction, say – but perhaps I'm being picky. I'm being similarly picky if I mention that I've never seen instructions before on how to hypnotise the deaf. The course blithely recommends using 'the deaf and dumb alphabet or if this is not understood then you write what you have to say'. Logical, I suppose.

At the back is a tear-off slip to enable you to obtain the higher course once you have completed all 36 lessons. Whoever owned the copy now living in the British Library obviously did not feel they had sufficiently mastered part one, and the slip remains intact. I think mine would have too.

Ormond McGill (1913–2005)

Ormond McGill wrote, in my opinion, *the* best book on stage hypnosis: *The New Encyclopedia of Stage Hypnotism*. In Fact, it's one of my favourite books on *any* topic *ever*! It consists of detailed accounts of how to do a whole range of stage acts, and it's exhaustive but never exhausting, because every page is filled with the most incredible info on things you never knew you wanted to know about hypnotising on stage. There are diagrams, things to make, what to whisper in the ears of your subjects, how the fakers get away with it … and much, much more. It even includes details on how to hypnotise a lobster (with diagrams).

I had lunch with the Dowager Duchess of Devonshire – Debo – twice, and it was a total delight. Her love of chickens was well documented, and she took my friend and I out to meet her chooks. I explained that Ormond McGill's book contained information on how to hypnotise a chicken. She laughed at this like a drain. I went on to explain that this was entirely a physiological process and nothing to do with hypnosis, and I was exhorted to 'stop spoiling it'. I sent her a thank-you card with a photocopy of Ormond's instructions, and received a reply saying that at her vast age she was delighted to have learned a new skill. I don't

believe in heaven, but I wish I did because the idea of Debo and Ormond laying out lines of stunned fowl somewhere in the never-never is worth dying to see.

HEROES OF HYPNOSIS
Pope Pius XII (1876–1958)

My candidate for most unlikely hypnotic hero is Pope Pius XII, in the Vatican during the Second World War. He's got a lot to answer for, but I'm not getting into any of that – the reason why he's Top of the Popes, hypnotically speaking, is that in 1956 he gave approval for the use of hypnosis following very strict guidelines. He pointed out that it was a serious business, and encouraging people to behave like chickens or pop stars was not approved of – but in some cases, such as in childbirth or for use as an anaesthetic, it was OK. This might not seem so shocking to us, but in 1956 this was a *big deal*, with some people at the time seeming to think this was like using a Ouija board to cure seasickness. However, I do like a hypnotic visionary; however outspoken, however much of a Pope-pourri (sorry!) his legacy may be.

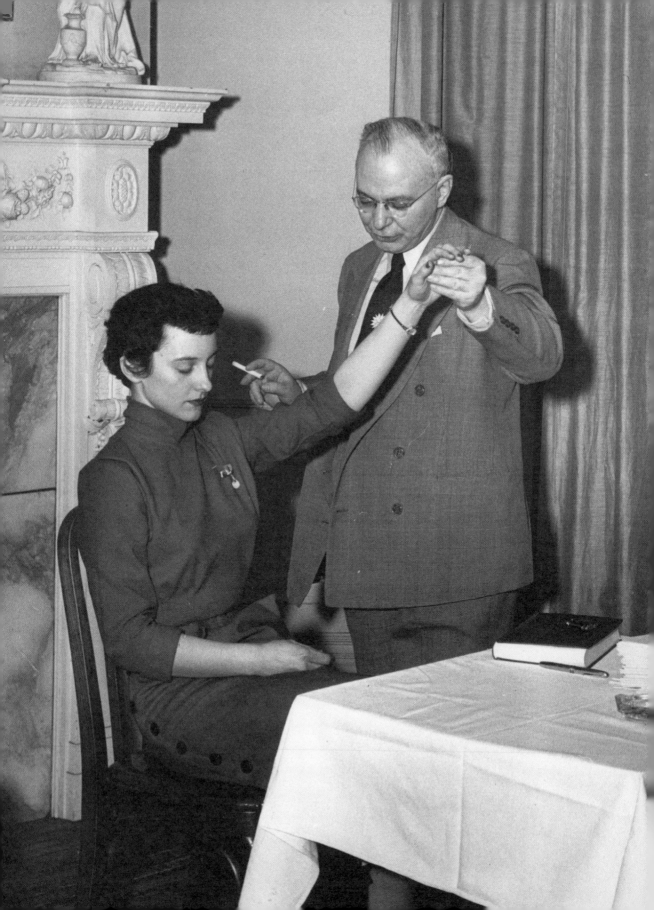

THE HISTORY

DECLINE AND RISE (AND RISE?)

In the twentieth century the great divide between science and showbiz continued. Popular entertainment circuits in many countries were full of stage hypnotists. Their routines broadly followed the same structure as those of the mesmerists, primarily presenting out-of-character behaviour, catalepsy, amnesia and inability to feel pain.

However, over in the world of therapeutic hypnosis, things weren't so cheery. Remember Bernheim? He was one of the leaders of the Nancy School. He was the one who said in 1897 'there's no such thing as hypnotism'.

He had stripped away all the layers of what hypnosis was, until he could only conclude that all that was going on was suggestion. This is what many people still believe; it doesn't matter as long as it is effective. At the same time Sigmund Freud, who had been an enthusiastic user of hypnosis in his consultations, began to reject the practice. He wasn't as stripped down about it all as Bernheim – he very much liked a good old-fashioned trance – but his ultimate rejection of the practice led to hypnosis existing outside of the mainstream for the next half-century. Maybe, and this is just a theory, it was actually necessary for all these doubting old men to die in order for new, exciting, playful ideas to come to prominence. Meanwhile, though, things were pretty dreary in the world of healing hypnosis.

However, though hypnotism was broadly rejected and out-of-favour in the mainstream, the two world wars were fertile periods for psychotherapeutic hypnosis. War, what it is good for? Quite a lot in terms of scientific, surgical and therapeutic advances, apparently. (Sorry for singing in the text. I'm unused to non-fiction. I'm sure it's frowned on in erudite circles.) There are stories from both wars about the use of hypnosis in the military, both for the treatment of trauma victims and – more thrillingly – as a tool in spying. But there was one person that you especially have to know about. He was the first unlikely sex-god of modern hypnosis, Milton H. Erickson (1902–1980). He swept away all the formal insistence

Dave Elman demonstrates an induction in 1951 at a medical hypnosis class. Famous for his relaxed manner and effortless pace, all summed up by his multi-tasking with a cigarette.

on standardised inductions, identical treatments and treating patients like laboratory subjects. Instead he created the personalised approach, in a highly naturalistic way. He was the master of the rapid induction. He developed the handshake induction, and used it so much that nobody wanted to shake his hand. Later on in his career he just seemed to be chatting to his clients, because the way he brought about hypnosis and the suggestions he gave were so informal. He was all about communicating with the unconscious, and this is pretty much what the practice is about today.

America went mental health crazy in the 1940s and 1950s, and hypnosis was ready for its turn in the limelight. It was ready for its close up and its teeth gleamed. Both in Hollywood movies and on the pages of the newspapers and scientific journals, hypnosis was big news.

This period led to the second golden age of hypnosis, starting sometime in the early 1960s, when research, theory and practice all thrived.

Overleaf is my pick of the pin-ups of this Golden Age.

Following the second golden age, hypnosis went through a dark period in the 1980s and 1990s, especially with regard to the use of the practice to uncover forgotten memories. That time was the start of our ongoing obsession with child abuse; the time of a changing morality and an increasing sense of responsibility. I think there was culturally a collective notion that it was better to risk social chaos than allow the vulnerable to be exploited. Very good you might say. Tear down the old structures and institutions that helped to protect the strong. However, in the midst of all this, hypnosis got itself into trouble. There were some practitioners who claimed they could help uncover forgotten memories. This is a highly dubious practice that is closer to past life regression than conventional hypnosis. It was so prominent in so many controversial cases that by the early 1990s a new term had been

---

America went mental health crazy in the 1940s and 1950s, and hypnosis was ready for its turn in the limelight. It was ready for its close-up and its teeth gleamed.

> **Hypnotism in the nineteenth century, broadly speaking, went from rigidity, to experimentation, to a golden age … and then plunged into obscurity. In the twentieth century it followed a similar pattern.**

coined – false memory syndrome. There was a lot of research which proved that it was possible to plant false memories in a subject – which is entirely logical if you think of hypnosis as being simply the power of suggestion. For a while it seemed that hypnosis was nothing more than dodgy stage routines and sinister clinicians keen on helping people get in touch with their subconscious, forgotten, memories. In reality there were only a small number of practitioners of this type, but they have cast a long shadow over the use of hypnosis. We are still very much in crisis over historical sexual abuse but it seems that hypnosis has dropped out of the picture. We don't need to complicate the story with meditation through techniques like hypnosis. A strong robust legal system is much more satisfying. Hypnotherapy again became known for its more benign uses, and the press let go of the hypnotic manipulative villain figure. Hypnosis entered the twenty-first century in pretty good, if perennially marginal, shape.

And so I've brought you, in my highly selective way, to the present day. I think of the history of hypnotism like this because it reveals a pattern that points to where the subject might be going in the future. Hypnotism in the nineteenth century, broadly speaking, went from rigidity, to experimentation, to a golden age … and then plunged into obscurity. In the twentieth century it followed a similar pattern. This might suggest that either we are in for a period where hypnosis snaps back into a tight, rigid definition and the whole process starts again – or there may be a fundamental seismic shift, like when mesmerism was first identified, or when mesmerism became hypnosis. I personally think a redefinition might be around the corner. I see it as a fusion of profound self-help techniques: it would be a mash-up of mindfulness, meditation and hypnosis, under a new name. It would also fill a huge need in our spiritual landscape and in our culture, and allow us to talk about our relationship with ourselves, our experiences of ourselves, and the stories we tell ourselves about our consciousness. It's exciting, isn't it?

Andrew Salter (1914–1996)

Founder of conditioned reflex therapy, Andrew Salter had a huge influence on the behavioural techniques of the twentieth century. I love him most for his virulent attacks on Sigmund Freud in particular, and psychoanalysis in general. I'd go so far as to say that he is so good that it's worth me going to the downstairs loo to seek out his book, to quote a classic line such as the one he opens with: 'It's high time that psychoanalysis, like the elephant of fable, dragged itself off to some distant jungle graveyard and died.'

Theodore R. Sarbin (1911–2005)

I like Theodore Sarbin because he developed the notion of 'role-taking'. This basically means that the subject is taking on the role of a different subject, and this produces the desired effects. It's acting 'as if'. It's the same as my questions in the introduction: 'How would it be if …?' As a performer I suppose I relate to this notion, but – if I can get a little abstract with you for a second – aren't we are all performers in almost every aspect of our own lives? This doesn't mean that we are inauthentic, but are simply going along with what Sarbin brilliantly called 'believed-in imaginings'.

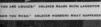

Andrew Salter was featured in *Life* magazine in 1941. This was a big deal even though the images owe as much to Hollywood as they do to science or therapy.

Theodore Barber (1927–2005)

Theodore Barber was influenced by Sarbin, but as a result of his extensive research he came to believe that hypnosis could have a huge effect regardless of the ability of the subject to go into hypnosis. That in fact, everyone has their own distinctive style, and the role of the practitioner is to help people find theirs. Like Bernheim decades before, back in Europe, Barber eventually concluded that mere suggestion was enough to create an effect. Spanos and Kirsch and many others later continued with this stripping away to get to the essentials of what was going on. This points the way towards a totally person-centric approach to hypnosis, which is what I believe in; that all a practitioner does is guide a client towards an understanding of their own relationship with hypnosis, and ultimately to an improved relationship with their own consciousness. It's all a long way from the helpless, passive recipients of mesmerism. Or, sadly, from the popular understanding of what goes on in hypnosis.

Irving Kirsch (1943–)

Kirsch is an expert on expectation and placebo. His research has indicated that throughout history, whenever hypnosis could be said to have worked the technique didn't matter; what mattered was the level of expectancy of the subject.

Dave Elman (1900–1967)

Elman was a great innovator. He was a quirky and playful yet influential hypnotist who stated that his aim was to bypass the critical faculty of the subject and bring about selective thinking. His influence mainly relates to the techniques for bringing about hypnosis. He was quick, and could teach students to bring about robust-enough hypnosis for surgical procedures in under three minutes. Under his instruction his students hypnotised the first patient to have heart surgery using hypnosis rather than anaesthesia. (This is hypno rock 'n' roll, and as such, I suggest we all lick his riff.)

Nicholas Spanos (1942–1994)

Spanos was a socio-cognitive hypnotist. He believed that the social context and the expectations of the hypnotist bring about results, even if they seem to the client to be involuntary. He did lots of work on dissociative identity disorder, which used to be called multiple personality disorder. Again, he deduced that hypnotism was a response to social pressure within a culture.

SEQUINS AND SPANDEX
THE STARS OF THE STAGE

OK You're up to date on all the fellas in suits who took hypnosis from the tailcoat through the sports jacket into the realm of the therapist (with no jacket) – but what about the ones in capes and shiny suits? The explosion of stage hypnotism during the twentieth century is best represented, I think, by looking at some of its most seductive stars.

These might not be the most famous, but they are the ones that shout loudly down the decades and grab the attention. And each one contributes something unique to the history of hypnotism – or at least a legendary moustache. I know this is entirely subjective, but you'll have realised by now that if you want an objective look at this subject you'll need to find a book by someone less giddy and interested in bright shiny things.

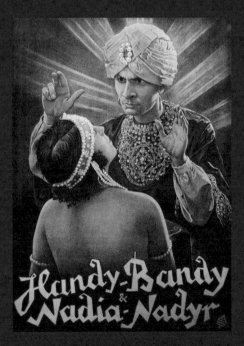

Handy-Bandy & Nadia-Nadyr

Opposite: Anonymous stage mentalist and mesmerist from 1910. This man is a call to arms for all stage hypnotists who go on stage in a T-shirt, ill-fitting suit or – heavens above – a bomber jacket. If I have interpreted it correctly, that reproachful stare is commanding us to 'make an effort'.

Left: Promotional poster for a German mystical stage act in 1927. All the fun of the East, and a suspiciously prissy turban. I wonder what happened to Handy and Nadia? I hope they were happy.

Above: The mesmeric hair of Bodie.

Right: Bodie flogging his product. Electric drugs. Now that is modern!

Below: The modestly named *Bodie Book*.

Walford Bodie, MD (1869–1939)

Walford Bodie spans the end of the period covered in the previous chapter, but then he also went on to dominate hypnosis until his death in 1939, so he feels very twentieth century to me. What a man! He was very much in the Karlyn mould, with stage electricity and bloodless surgery. He drove people crazy – and often into courtrooms – because he insisted on using the MD after his name. He claimed this stood for 'Merry Devil' when pressed, and not 'Medical Doctor' at all – silly! He was also the inheritor of Karlyn's moustache crown. Bodie's is the dominant moustache in modern hypnotic history. He was Britain's highest-paid entertainer at the time, and this comes as no surprise when you read about his electric chair act. He was a trained electrician, so he knew what he was doing – you would hope. I don't think it would get past a modern risk assessment, though. He famously said 'there's more money in shocking and terrifying than in edifying' – sad but true. Without him the modern stage hypnotism routine wouldn't exist as we know it today, from the most jaw-dropping moments to the corniest gags.

Bodie's early book from 1905 is very revealing of the man and – given that we *are* talking 1905, the heyday of Freud's new theories – his enormous ego. Walford Bodie was never one to hide himself away. His book is called *The Bodie Book*. It features many pictures of him and his stonking moustache. There's also a picture of Mrs Walford Bodie, who looks

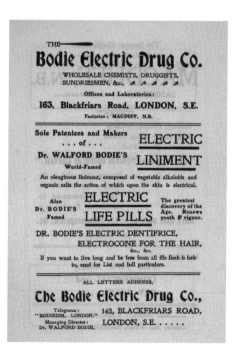

Before Treatment.
THE PATIENT CANNOT LIFT HALF-AN-OUNCE.

After Treatment.
THE PATIENT LIFTS HALF-A-HUNDREDWEIGHT.

The age-old story – help a man with a withered arm gain miraculous strength but lose your hat in the process. Who hasn't been there?

remarkably like Bodie himself in a wig and a slightly smaller moustache. Also a picture of Miss Marie Walford (Mystic Marie). She is what my grandmother called a 'handsome woman', by which she meant 'a bit rough'. Bodie explains his lack of modesty in naming this *The Bodie Book*: 'I call it *The Bodie Book* because it is an exposition of Bodiesism or the art of healing by Bodic Force.' He modestly goes on to explain that 'Bodic force is my peculiar discovery. Franklyn tamed the lightning; Morse taught it the English language; I have instructed it in anatomy and physiology and endowed it with intelligent sympathy.' Even if these clues weren't enough, I think you might have got the measure of him by the time you reach Chapter 13, which is called 'What the Papers Say About Me'. Nothing bad, apparently.

For all this posturing, however, Bodie's book is quite beautifully written:

'All know the word Hypnotism. They have heard it bandied about in joke and cheap common-place. They have seen it made the subject of illustrations and jests in comic papers, and have been led by the spirit of the modern age to regard it as a comprehensive term used to describe humbug and collusion in a non-committal way … Some … are easily persuaded by sceptics that it is composed of two parts trickery and one part glamour.' The fact that 'two parts trickery and one part glamour' perfectly sums up Bodie himself was an irony that the man was no doubt aware of.

Naturally Bodie, like the mesmerist Burrows before him, had his own range of products. His, naturally enough, given his obsession with electricity, had extra voltage and were recommended 'If you want to live long and be free from all ills flesh is heir to'. The Bodie Electric Drug Company sold many useful-sounding products, including Bodie's Electric Liniment and Bodie's Electric Life Pills.

> '**We were marvellous Svengalis or Dr Mesmers,**
> **engaged in a supernatural practice of sorts.**
> **Then it all collapsed. For me anyway.**'

Kreskin before his change of heart, adding to the confusion around hypnosis with the old clichés of fob watch, hypnotic stare and mesmeric hand.

The Amazing Kreskin (1935–)

Kreskin (born George Joseph Kresge) is still with us. He is a mentalist and hypnotist who first became famous on US TV in the 1970s. The range of his dodgy techniques, including telepathy, clairvoyance and precognition, had a lot to answer for in terms of creating public confusion as to

THE BASIC PRINCIPLES OF KRESKIN'S ESP

what hypnosis actually is. However, he was always damned entertaining, and even wore capes.

Mid-career his story got more interesting. He had begun to doubt that the hypnotic trance state really existed. He said: 'For nineteen years I had believed in … the sleep like "hypnotic trance", practicing it constantly. Though I had nagging doubts at times, I wanted to believe in it. There was an overpowering mystique about putting someone to sleep, something that set me and all other "hypnotists" apart. We were marvelous Svengalis or Dr. Mesmers, engaged in a supernatural practice of sorts. Then it all collapsed. For me anyway.'

So he started performing stage hypnosis without any induction, thereby moving on our understanding of the subject as being – as I've said many times in this book – simply a response to suggestion. I think he's right in believing that this makes hypnosis much more powerful than just something that one person can do to another. Its possibilities are profound. As an old man he doesn't seem to wear capes anymore, which is a shame, but he is still a major figure in this world.

Douglas Watson

The photograph shows mass hypnotism at Enfield – this is a long way from the London Palladium, and I love it for that. Here Douglas Watson is photographed photographing his subjects. This is a weird hypnotic selfie, and surely the first – and possibly last – of its kind. It's also unusual to see this arrangement of chairs; usually they are all in a line. Douglas Watson is not a famous stage hypnotist, but the camera never lies – he looks very effective doesn't he?

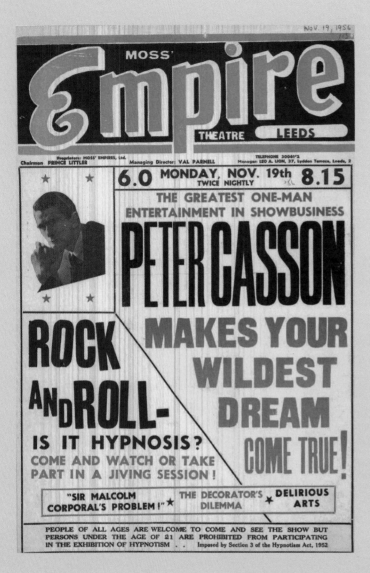

MOSS' **Empire** THEATRE LEEDS

Nov. 19, 1956

Proprietors: MOSS' EMPIRES, Ltd.
Chairman PRINCE LITTLER   Managing Director: VAL PARNELL
TELEPHONE 30061/2
Manager: LEO A. LION, 37, Lyddon Terrace, Leeds, 2

6.0 MONDAY, NOV. 19th **8.15**
TWICE NIGHTLY

THE GREATEST ONE-MAN
ENTERTAINMENT IN SHOWBUSINESS

PETER CASSON
MAKES YOUR WILDEST DREAM COME TRUE!

ROCK AND ROLL —
IS IT HYPNOSIS?
COME AND WATCH OR TAKE
PART IN A JIVING SESSION!

"SIR MALCOLM CORPORAL'S PROBLEM!" ★ THE DECORATOR'S DILEMMA ★ DELIRIOUS ARTS

PEOPLE OF ALL AGES ARE WELCOME TO COME AND SEE THE SHOW BUT
PERSONS UNDER THE AGE OF 21 ARE PROHIBITED FROM PARTICIPATING
IN THE EXHIBITION OF HYPNOTISM . .   Imposed by Section 3 of the Hypnotism Act, 1952

Note the reference to the recent Stage Hypnotism Act. This bill is a nice attempt to knit together rock and roll and hypnosis.

Peter Casson (1921–1995)

Peter Casson was Walford Bodie's natural successor, but without any of his flamboyance. In the immediate postwar period he became a big variety star; so much so, in fact, that he was invited to perform his stage show on the BBC at Alexandra Palace. The story goes that his act was so successful that he hypnotised several engineers in the control booth – and the BBC, as the world's first mass broadcaster, understandably got a little worried. That wasn't his only problem, though. His ubiquity and success led to popular campaigns to control stage shows like his. This came to a head with a court case involving an American hypnotist in the UK called Ralph Slater. Casson and Slater's practices are felt to have influenced the government to act, which it did by introducing the Hypnotism Act in 1952 – still the legal framework that controls hypnotism today. Ironically Casson went on to form his own organisation in the 1970s, called the Federation of Ethical Stage Hypnotists. He was worried by the rise of what he saw as unscrupulous stage hypnotists. He doesn't seem to have been very showbiz-y, very flamboyant or very much fun from the glimpses he has left behind in the archives, but he definitely added a lot to the history of stage hypnotism. Whether he lived up to his advertised promises – 'Makes your wildest dreams come true!' and 'The greatest one-man entertainment in showbizness' – is anyone's guess. Mine would be … probably not.

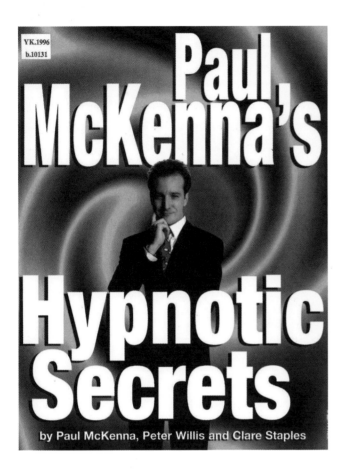

Paul McKenna's Hypnotic Secrets

by Paul McKenna, Peter Willis and Clare Staples

McKenna is the king of self-help hypnosis, and the most successful hypnotist ever. He has fused the science and the showbiz in the mainstream, and made a tidy profit in doing so.

Paul McKenna (1963–)

McKenna is the king of self-help hypnosis, and the most successful hypnotist ever. He has fused the science and the showbiz in the mainstream, and made a tidy profit in doing so. Starting as a stage hypnotist, he developed a successful but fairly conventional act. A defining moment in his career came when he was sued by a participant in one of his stage shows, back when he was a regular cheesy stage hypnotist in 1998. The participant claimed that he had been made into an 'aggressive schizophrenic'. His clever barrister got him off with the counter-intuitive defense that McKenna couldn't have done this by inducing the hypnotic state, because the hypnotic state doesn't exist. The description of the show illustrates perfectly what I was talking about in terms of the stage hypnosis routine differing little from the mesmeric demonstrations of the 1860s.

McKenna had already started studying with Richard Bandler, the co-founder of neuro-linguistic programming (NLP). By combining his populist style with the principles of NLP he has sold millions of books and audiobooks, many of which are in a series called *I Can Make You …* He represents the ultimate fusion of the science and the showbiz of hypnosis.

Anatoly Kashpirovsky (1939–)

The astonishing and – speaking entirely personally – rather worrying, Anatoly Kashpirovsky is a Russian hypnotist and psychic healer. He is also a one-time Russian politician. (You can tell he was a Russian politician because he is often pictured without a shirt.) The mass hypnotism demonstration pictured here is entirely possible for any practictioner to achieve. I did it once while singing people into a hypnotic reverie but the members of the audience, being mainly British, weren't totally delighted to be lying on the floor crumpling their best outfits. I notice this stage is carpeted, so maybe even a Russian audience in the 1980s wasn't as hardcore as we might have supposed.

Here too is Kashpirovsky encouraging a woman to dance. It reeks of 1989 and the dying days of communism – but take away the big crowd, put the woman in a boob tube and give the hypnotist a pint and you could be in a pub in Swansea with the girl pretending to be Kate Bush.

Derren Brown (1971–)

It is entirely fitting, considering the smoke-and-mirrors aspect of this subject, that the most famous British hypnotist of our time isn't really a hypnotist at all. Hypnotism is simply one of a range of showbiz tricks that he employs to create his shows. He is a showman with a love of many forms of carefully researched mysterious showbiz entertainments, which are lovingly incorporated into new routines. But his experiments with what looks like mind-altering thought control and Russian roulette, and so on, are what most people first think of in the UK when hypnosis is mentioned. Which probably isn't very useful if they would just like to stop biting their nails.

A generic-looking poster for a generic-sounding act. 'Barnum' is unlikely to be have been what his mama called him, and he is nothing to do with the famous Phineas Thomas Barnum. The act apparently features a human bridge that would actually kill the subject, even if you could get four men standing side by side on one body. There's also lots of musical nonsense, amateur dental work, fishing in a chamber pot and a man proposing romantic love to another man. Barnum called that a show. I'd call that a quiet Saturday night in.

MY STORY
PART 2

I **ran away with myself at the end of the last chapter about my relationship with hypnosis. (I'll never be Agatha Christie. I'd get over-excited and you'd know who the murderer was by Chapter 3.) So, we were at the stage where I'd stumbled across hypnosis and gone on a one-day course.**

It might surprise you to learn that many doctors, nurses and therapists study hypnosis as part of their training, to add to their skills base. If you're having minor surgery, or dental work, or anything that makes you uneasy, I've found that hypnosis will often change the mood. The practitioner themselves will either know nothing about it but be mildly interested, or they might have studied it but feel shy about making it part of their approach with patients – which is a shame. However, a little bit of self-hypnosis goes a very long way when someone is bearing down on you with a needle. The ability to take yourself to a sunny place where the pain can happen but doesn't worry you is a useful skill to have – well worth the price of this book. (Having said that, a very stressed consultant in the process of removing a fragment of my face for a skin biopsy once snapped at me 'Are

you meditating?' 'I'm using self-hypnosis,' I replied, from a place of peace and tranquillity. 'Oh God!' she barked. We didn't get into a detailed discussion.

I'm partly telling you the story of my adventures in hypnosis-land to make it clear that this is a subject that will reward you for making your own. It thrives on personal study. The big characters mentioned in this book have learned a little from others and then incorporated it into their own therapy, or their own performance or – most significantly – their own everyday lives. You can learn what other people have done, and you can learn some tricks and techniques, but ultimately it's about what *you* do with it. Don't think that there's a right way and a wrong way. You're not being taught how to bake a sponge cake. You're being taught to make an oven, mill the flour and invent the cake that is perfect just for you.

Looking back on it, it seems a little radical to me that as a busy performer with not much free time, I would embark on a lengthy diploma course in cognitive behavioural hypnotherapy. It was certainly a long time since I had sat in a classroom situation. But at the start of that first day, I came across the statement from the introduction: 'Everything human beings do is habit, and all habit can change.' I couldn't let that go. The implications of it were too huge to contemplate. I was already used to the fact that so much that we do is beyond our control, is driven by nature or other people, and that I was pretty disempowered. I kept thinking of things: 'Falling in love!' I'd cry, and the tutor would patiently explain that he considered falling in love to be a good thing, but that it was something we reinforced with our behaviour every day. We wake up and think 'This is the person I love!', and when they are lovely we think 'I love them because they behave like this!'

Everything human beings do is habit, and all habits can change.

and all the time the neural pathways are getting stronger (and are only weakened when you attempt to get something from the marketplace in IKEA together and you start to change that thought habit). The tutor didn't actually mention IKEA, but he was very patient with me as I kept pushing up against the limitations of my worldview as it existed then. I was on the course with lots of therapists, and I think this notion wasn't such big news to them. It makes sense that they would have had a bigger understanding of the potential for change, as this would seem to be a basic requirement of their job. So much so that some of them seemed quite bored, while I was giddily reeling from excitement. I now see that an understanding of the potential for change is a basic requirement for *my* job. I have always preached through the comedy pulpit about the necessity for change, and now I profoundly believe in it. I'm not calling for revolution, but for us to entertain the notion that change is always an option available to us. Entertaining that possibility is what entertainment is.

I loved getting to be the one that people practised on. It's a great feeling when you allow yourself to go into that extended, structured, playful state several times a day, even when someone is stumbling over a printed script. I also liked being the one doing the hypnotising. (I'm versatile, thanks for asking.) Both are a little bit like a performance, so I was comfortable. Of course I made mistakes; I still cringe about the time I was working with someone who was afraid of sweating in public. During the deepening of hypnosis phase of the process I was getting lyrical and poetic. I told him that relaxation would run through him like a river. (What does that even mean?) Anyway, it was the wrong image. Almost immediately I saw beads of sweat start to form on his brow, and by the time I was bringing him out of hypnosis he was drenched. 'Was the river not a helpful image?' I asked. He shook his head, and sweat flew off him as he did so. I felt a fool.

I was lucky in my teacher. He was into philosophy, personal development and above all making this practice into what you wanted it to be. He liked the fact that I was a performer, while everyone else in the class was a therapist of some kind. So much of hypnosis is acting 'as if'. If 'acting' weren't a slightly pejorative word, with connotations of inauthenticity, the idea of it could be used to great benefit. 'Whenever I feel afraid, I hold my head erect, and whistle a happy tune, and no one would suspect, I'm afraid.' (Sorry – I broke into song there, which we have established is OK in cabaret and rude in non-fiction. But you get the point.) You could argue that we're always acting; the skill lies in learning to change the script.

In the middle of this process I decided I wanted to learn stage hypnosis too. The whole thing felt like four days in a cheap conference centre during the foundation of an ill-fated right-wing political party that made UKIP look like the SDP. But I did take the advice given on the course, including the profound comment 'you'd be surprised what people will do if you ask them nicely', added some gags, and started performing the routine as stage hypnotist Derek Diamond. So, though I got a chill in my soul, I got a bloody good act out of it.

"AU CLAIR DE LA LUNE"

HYPNOSIS IN
POPULAR CULTURE

Much of this book is about hypnosis on a variety of stages: illegitimate and legitimate; scholarly, scientific and medical; and from the trashy and trite to the elevated and erudite. However, it is not on stage, but on screen – large and small – that much of the myth making around hypnosis has occurred.

Before we get into that and I start using the word 'tropes' a lot, I'd ask you to consider this thought: Perhaps there is a natural affinity between form and content with on-screen drama and hypnosis. I'd argue that sitting in the dark, or sitting on your sofa staring at either your TV or your laptop, is to enter into a hypnotic pact. (If you accept this proposition then we should all start screaming right this very second.) These days the greatest part of our time is spent indulging in screen-staring, and it is fundamentally teaching our brains to turn off the active functioning capacity that has served us very well for thousands of years. I'm a big fan of my frontal lobe, and I'd like to keep it packing as much of a punch as possible, thank you, but I willingly command it to give up its power every time I sit down to watch small children falling over or something about Postmodernism (obviously this is

because I only watch camcorder shows and elevating educational documentaries).

Dr Aric Sigman wrote a fantastic book about the hypnotic power of TV called *Remotely Controlled*. In his brilliantly titled essay 'Weapons of Mass Induction', he quotes findings from Prof. Herbert Krugman in the early 1970s that claim that it takes around 30 seconds for television to induce a brain state similar to the brain under hypnosis. We kind of know this ourselves, don't we? We refer to 'vegging out' in front of the TV. Isn't that why the TV is always on in old people's homes, hospital waiting rooms, sexual health clinics and prisons? It's a cheap form of social control. I know this view of mass media is hardly original, but its relationship to hypnosis is, I think, and I wonder whether this is why hypnosis refuses to lay down and die – perhaps because we are mass consuming hypnosis on a daily basis?

Nobody could blame Trilby for falling under the sway of Svengali. His hypnotic stare, combined with an astonishing one-piece beard and hair combination, would send anyone into a spin.

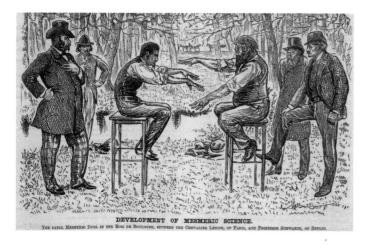

DEVELOPMENT OF MESMERIC SCIENCE.
THE FATAL MESMERIC DUEL IN THE BOIS DE BOULOGNE, BETWEEN THE CHEVALIER LENOIR, OF PARIS, AND PROFESSOR SCHWARTZ, OF BERLIN.

"'ET MAINTENANT DORS, MA MIGNONNE!'"

Above left: A cartoon by George du Maurier from *Punch*, 1883.

Above right: One of du Maurier's original illustrations for Trilby.

Opposite: Following the publication of du Maurier's *Trilby*, the public went Svengali-crazy in the 1890s. The novel spawned stage adaptations, songs and this waltz to be played in the privacy of your own parlour. Note the evil Svengali at the piano, and the somnambulistic stare of Trilby.

This may have been what Pierre Janet was anticipating with his famous quote in 1919: 'Hypnosis is quite dead – until the day of its resurrection.' For him the new media of film was the resurrection, and it has certainly thrived ever since.

Even the briefest and most quirkily subjective trot through the history of hypnosis in popular culture has to focus on the figure of Svengali, created by the writer and illustrator George du Maurier. Now here was a man extremely interested in hypnosis – above left is a cartoon he drew for *Punch* in 1883.

Eleven years later du Maurier published his best-known work, *Trilby*. The story of the evil, sinister, controlling Svengali turning the tone-deaf innocent Trilby into an automaton and an internationally famous opera singer provided the template for the hypnotists that followed. The aggressive anti-Semitism hasn't stuck around, thankfully, but much else in the novel has, from the notion of the innocent controlled by a figure of evil, to the name of a jaunty hat. Du Maurier's twin creative roles of writer and illustrator are equally important here; the aesthetic is embedded into the narrative at every point. This is probably why the story transferred so well to a visual medium once this was technically possible.

Immediately there were very successful stage versions, with the first in London in 1895 staring no less a celebrity than Sir Herbert Beerbohm Tree, famous actor and theatre manager. By the following year there was a parody called *Drilby*, and it is reckoned there were at least 24 different adaptations playing simultaneously in America. The manifestation of 'trilbyana' included sausages, ice cream, jewellery and shoes, as well as the eponymous hat. But significantly, the novel became an international sensation just as the medium of film was getting going. There have been many film adaptations since, with John Barrymore's 1931 starring turn as Svengali perhaps being the most influential.

It's noteworthy that most of these films are called *Svengali* rather than *Trilby*. Du Maurier's victim has become anonymous – just a hat, not a person – rather than a victim of crime; the perpetrator has meanwhile been immortalised.

Following in Svengali's sinister footsteps come almost a century's worth of hypnotic

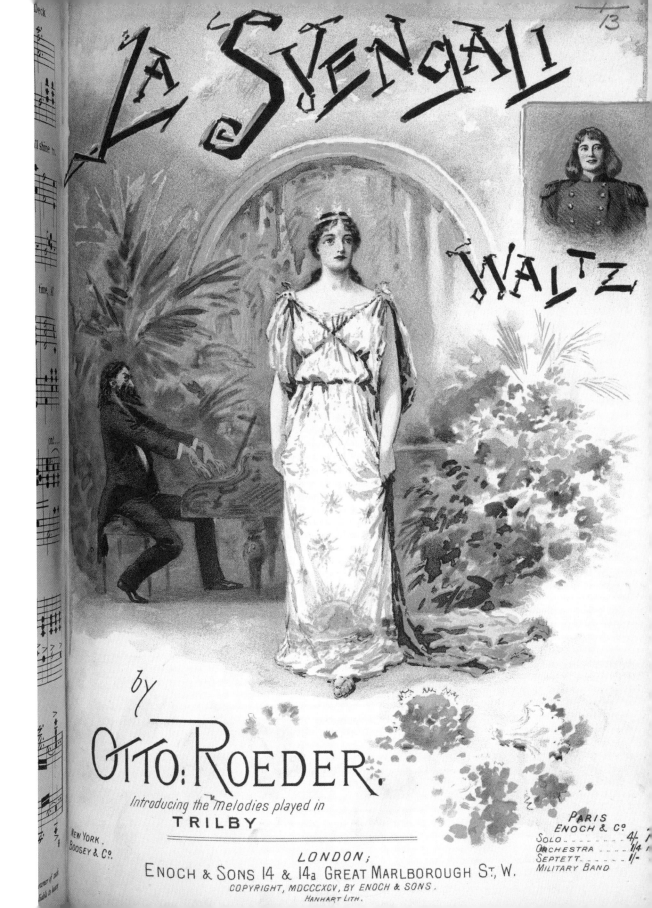

La Svengali

Waltz

by

Otto Roeder.

Introducing the melodies played in
TRILBY

NEW YORK.
Boosey & C°

PARIS
ENOCH & C°
SOLO 4/-
ORCHESTRA 4/4
SEPTETT 4/4
MILITARY BAND ... 1/-

LONDON;
ENOCH & SONS 14 & 14a GREAT MARLBOROUGH S⸀ W.
COPYRIGHT, MDCCCXCV, BY ENOCH & SONS.
HANHART LITH.

baddies. If there's a hypnotist in a film, you can bet your popcorn that nothing good will come of it. They are either evil manipulators, or evil seducers, or both. And in the case of Danny Boyle's 2012 film *Trance*, they are a seducer, a manipulator *and* a woman to boot. Which can only be worse.

These figures are so powerful because each builds on the one that precedes him (it's usually a him). So with just a whiff of the hypnotic we can guess at the aesthetic that will follow: darkness, piercing gazes, a swinging watch or two, hypnotic spirals, hushed intense voices … It has its own momentum, exactly in the way that the Dracula myth does. Svengali's descendants are as prolific and varied as Dracula's, but there's one big difference between them. Listen up all of you (even goths – and I'm sorry to break this to you): vampires ain't real, but hypnosis very much is. So in every audience of a hypnosis film, there will be a certain percentage who should shout 'Hang

on a minute, this is nonsense. Hypnosis helped me!' OK, I know a Hollywood film isn't a documentary; I'm not completely naive. I know that the showbiz meme of the hypnotist has grown like a mutating virus until it is unrecognisable from its antecedents, and a long, long way away from the pragmatic reality. (I don't think there are many movies to be made about curing dog phobias.) So is that OK then? Does the public at large understand that the trope is just that, an entertainment tradition that has nothing to do with reality? I don't think they do. They think it's the truth. Which is exactly what – if you'll excuse me a soapbox moment – is wrong with film and television industries all over the world. Namely that, as a default, they would rather entertain us than tell us the truth. I want to be entertained, yes, but above all I want the truth. We're not alive long enough to pay to be lied to.

I'd say that these evil on-screen manipulators fall into two camps: the first is squarely in the Svengali mode. 'Evil man controlling hapless victim' has popped up again and again in the decades that followed *Trilby*, such as in *The Hypnotic Eye* in 1947, the Italian film *Hipnosis* in

---

If there's a hypnotist in a film, you can bet your popcorn that nothing good will come of it. They are either evil manipulators, or evil seducers, or both.

1963 and the bizarre Korean movie *The Hypnotised (Eolguleobtneun Minyeo)* from 2004. In this shocker a psychiatrist seduces his former patient into doing all sorts of things that she wouldn't otherwise do. She has a really terrible time. I don't want to dismiss a film with an overblown statement that may be out of all proportion in relation to its cultural significance, but it is everything that is wrong with the patriarchy.

The other camp features the hypnotist who forces innocents to commit murder, and this has remained a favourite right up to the present day. It can be traced

back to the German expressionist classic *The Cabinet of Dr Caligari* from 1920, in which Dr Caligari controls a fairground somnambulist whom he sends out at night to commit dreadful murders. But actually it is all a dream, and Dr Caligari is really a murderous psychiatrist. These themes of the man who is trained to help, but who encourages the vulnerable to trust him and his strange therapies, keeps recurring. I love *Fear in the Night* from 1947, which has noirish feel and all the strangeness you would expect from a film with a sinister hypnotist at its heart. It's low-rent – which

1960s horror flick *The Hypnotic Eye*, introducing that new innovation HypnoMagic, which was, in reality, getting the audience to join in with the hypnotic bits themselves. Experiential cinema! Love it.

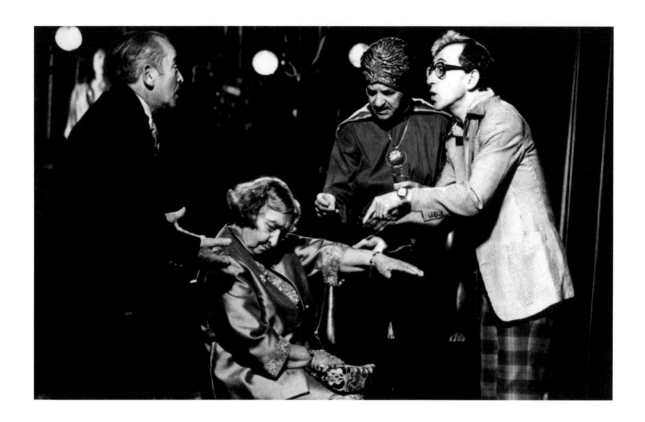

A still from Woody Allen's film *Broadway Danny Rose* (1984). Here, the dodgy stage hypnotist has got a lady stuck in an arm levitation. Allen returned to the comic potential of hypnotism in *The Curse of the Jade Scorpion* in 2001, which is all about a hypnotist using his powers to get people to do evil things (you'll not be surprised to learn).

you might guess, because it is based on a short story by Cornell Woolrich with the criminal pun in the title 'And So To Death' – but it's well worth a watch.

Perhaps the most salacious film of this type was made in 1960, in a period when America was crazy for hypnotism following the Bridey Murphy case (more of which later). *The Hypnotic Eye* was about a stage hypnotist who gave hot women in his audience the suggestion to mutilate themselves. The stage sections were overseen by the stage hypnotist and hypnotic guru Gil Boyne (1924–2010), which means they are very credible. If it weren't for the fact that it pushes the age-old fiction that all hypnotists use the practice for their own evil intents it would be pretty authentic. This was enhanced by

the use of a new screen process called Hypnomagic ('It makes YOU part of the show!'). It's all very immersive, because suddenly we are out of the plot and being encouraged to experience hypnotism for ourselves. This bit I find very exciting – so much so that it's been a direct influence on my Singing Hypnotist show, especially the balloon-that-turns-into-lead segment. However, I don't have a mechanical hypnotic eye in my right hand – which seems like nothing but an oversight, now I come to think of it. Talking of recycling and there being nothing new under the sun, *The Hypnotic Eye* was pretty much the basis for *Saimin* (1999) a Japanese horror movie in which it turns out that a hypnotherapist is inducing people to commit suicide. (Oops, spoiler alert!) There's a nice touch in that

Freud curing Sherlock Holmes of addiction and an obsession with Moriarty, from the 1976 film *The Seven-Per-Cent Solution*. You know that you are bound to be in for a riot of factual inaccuracies when you get a fictional character asking for treatment from a historical one.

a key plot point is for all the suicides to mention 'green monkey' before they die. Very stage hypnotist, that.

If you want a portrait of a less evil hypnotist, look to *The Seventh Veil* (1945). Admittedly he is played by Herbert Lom, one of the most sinister-looking actors in the history of cinema. He is treating a suicidal character played by Ann Todd, and helps her to uncover the root of her problems using a series of flashbacks. It's a very useful device for the screen, the flashback – beautifully filmic, but not very truthful in terms of what happens in hypnosis … but then you can't have everything. He didn't horribly butcher people, at least; what more do you want?

It's tempting to hypothosise that the twentieth century was the period of

human history when the dark side of the human psyche revealed itself. Psychiatry was one of the weapons against such forces of evil. But could those men who walked on the wild side of the mind really be trusted? The year that *Trilby* was written, 1894, was the same year that Sigmund Freud tried cocaine. Can the healers really be relied on? Popular culture is still very invested in telling us that, as far as hypnotists are concerned, the answer is 'no'.

Before we get serious, I'd like to mention a couple of cinematic curiosities. *Heart of Glass* is a film made in 1976 by Werner Herzog. It's set in a glass factory in eighteenth-century Bavaria (so you know it's going to rock). It's famous in hypnotic circles (or should that be spirals?) because Herzog reputedly had all the

The 1936 British film *The Man Who Could Work Miracles*, staring Roland Young, is a nice antidote to all the gloom of the evil hypnotist. He's a hapless guy who suddenly realises he can do whatever he wants. Here he is removing a plain shopgirl's unwanted freckles. The shopgirl is played by Joan 'Miss Marple' Hickson (her big line is "Ow 'e dunnit, I dunno!'). Young's character isn't really a hypnotist, or a magician. HG Wells – who wrote the original story – is clearly playing with the idea of those figures and recasting them as someone low-status who doesn't want the bother of it all. I like the idea of the reluctantly powerful … in nice contrast to virtually everyone else in these pages (me included, naturally).

actors hypnotised every day of shooting. Sometimes Debbie Harry and Chris Stein of Blondie claim they took the title of their 1978 smash disco epic from the movie. (Other times, they deny it.) The film itself is a strange watch; despite the fact that my eyes felt like they had been scraped against sandpaper by the end of it because it was so boring, the film is an unlikely high point in the history of filmed hypnosis.

Meanwhile, Lars Von Trier tried to hypnotise the entire audience with his 1991 film *Europa*. The introductory narration is a fake hypnotic induction, and at the end the voice instructs the audience to wake up. It's a brilliant device – and, as I said at the start of this section, a logical marriage of the form and content of filmed entertainment and hypnosis. He is simply making explicit what everything from the nightly news

to *Cash in the Attic* does covertly.

Television has consistently misunderstood hypnosis throughout its history, representing it as something that someone does to someone else (usually for evil purposes), rather than simply a change in the perspective of the person who is hypnotised. Which is strange, because the ability to change the way we see the world is a much more profound thing that a nasty person doing something nasty. Virtually every one of those formulaic shows, from *Murder She Wrote*, via *Hart to Hart* to *Scooby-Doo*, where they have to come up with a baddie per episode, will have an evil hypnotist pop up from time to time. For example, witness the show where Columbo worked out that a suicide thought she was diving into a swimming pool, not off a tall building –

because she had been hypnotised. My favourite show from the 1970s, *Wonder Woman*, had more than its fair share of these characters. In 1975 Diana Prince is hypnotised by a man with a bubble perm and wearing a kipper tie into betraying her secrets. But Wonder Woman isn't that naïve. Diana may have looked like she was a victim, but the sly sexy smile that made Lynda Carter one of the decade's biggest stars told us better, and she was twirling in an explosion before you could say 'back in the room'.

And talking about Back in the Room – that's the title of a new British TV trashy entertainment show in which people

---

Television has consistently misunderstood hypnosis throughout its history, representing it as something that someone does to someone else (usually for evil purposes), rather than simply a change in the perspective of the person who is hypnotised.

---

compete to be hypnotised. It's all great fun, but repeat after me, not hypnosis in any real sense. You *can* combine the science and the showbiz but it seems most people don't try. Maybe prime time Saturday evening light entertainment was never going to be the place it thrived. Shame. Ormond McGill could have made it work, Walford Bodie could have, but they have the slight disadvantage of being dead and therefore less likely to get the commission.

So the movies, aided and abetted by television, are a major part of the smoke and mirrors of hypnosis. They are what makes the subject so readily accessible to us now. So easy to understand, so immediate. And yet so very, very wrong. They help to confuse most of the people who turn up at the door of a clinical hypnotherapist, and they provide much of the white-noise nonsense of the stage hypnotist. It's surprising that modern films and TV still trot out the tired clichés as much as they ever did but, as I've said, it's got a life of its own now. It's true because it's become the truth, despite the fact that it's a lie. The fictional Svengali is much more real in the popular imagination than the real heroes of hypnosis.

Sheet Music
'How I Mesmerise 'Em'

I discovered this sheet music tucked away in the British Library basements. It was part of my increasingly fevered search for hypnotists who sang. I was convinced that in the intersection between the science and showbiz there must have been singing hypnotists. Logical, right? Except it didn't happen. Not until I became the Singing Hypnotist in 2012.

There are a couple of other comic songs about hypnosis, including the American vaudeville song 'Svengali in Disguise'. This tells various stories about how people use hypnosis to get what they want, from the snake in the Garden of Eden, to a fat girl getting a seat on a bus. It's not subtle, but it's a damned fun sing. It was written by Harry Von Tilzer, who was Judy Garland's uncle. It reveals the extent of the cultural dominance of the Trilby/Svengali story – it's naturally assumed that the listener knows all about them.

But my favourite is this classic, 'How I Mesmerise 'Em', from 1891 – the tale of a bloke who tries to mesmerise his wife.

First I tickle her under the chin
That seemed to make her smile
Then I gave her a dig in the ribs
(she was laughing all the while)
I waved my hands all over her face
Did a gentle creep
Then I gave a tap on the jaw with this
(shows clenched fist)
*And she went righ*t off to sleep.

So domestic violence – presumably always hilarious – is the way to do it, rather than go to the bother of mesmerising. He moves on to do the same to his landlord's rent collector, a burglar who breaks in one night, and finally a policeman who tries to arrest him and his mate for being drunk and disorderly. A thoroughly disreputable character, clearly, but the fact that a comic song takes for granted that everyone understood the basics of hypnosis – the mesmeric passes hands over the face, the gentle creep – shows how ingrained in society it was.

23

How I Mesmerise 'Em

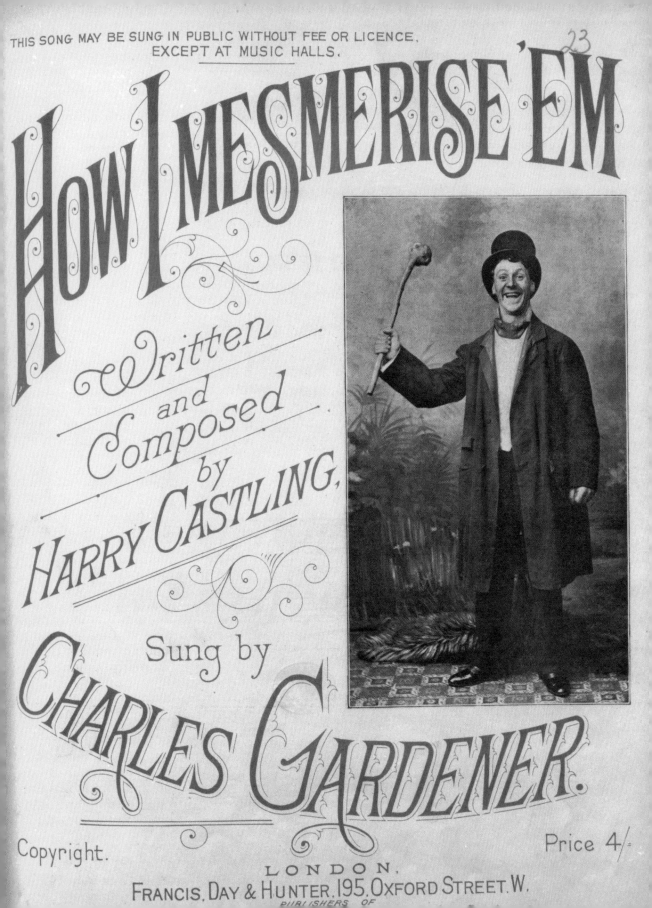

Written and Composed by

Harry Castling,

Sung by

Charles Gardener.

Copyright.

Price 4/-

LONDON,
Francis, Day & Hunter, 195, Oxford Street, W.
PUBLISHERS OF

A FULL DISCOVERY

OF THE

STRANGE PRACTICES

OF

Dr. ELLIOTSON

On the bodies of his

FEMALE PATIENTS!

AT HIS HOUSE, IN CONDUIT STREET, HANOVER SQ.

WITH ALL THE SECRET

EXPERIMENTS HE MAKES UPON THEM,

AND THE

Curious Postures they are put into while sitting or standing, when awake or asleep!

A female Patient being blindfolded, to undergo an operation.

THE WHOLE AS SEEN

BY AN EYE-WITNESS,

AND NOW FULLY DIVULGED!

&c. &c. &c.

I'm so glad to see that this isn't titillating in the slightest. The language is so revealing: 'on the bodies of his female patients'. Not on the women, you understand, but on their bodies. And why does it take place 'at his house' … and why is there an 'eye-witness' who must 'divulge'? It's all very prurient and unpleasant and doesn't exactly inspired confidence in the medical practices of the good doctor. I take exactly no comfort from the line of 'etc.'s at the bottom. They can bode NO GOOD.

WOMEN AND HYPNOSIS

As we've noted, the history of hypnosis is full of women. Full of women wordlessly fainting, swooning and lying prone while men do the business on them, that is. They are usually nameless, sub-Trilby figures, merely glimpsed in illustrations and photographs.

I performed at a conference for hypnotherapists once, and there was a man speaking who claimed that he could make women's breasts bigger with hypnosis. The evidence was slight and the demand for his treatment seemed even more slight, but what was most fascinating was the way that almost all the male attendees couldn't see anything wrong with this, while most of the women did. The notion of a man encouraging a woman to change part of their body through HypnoGrowth is entirely antithetical to the reason why most women want to get into hypnotherapy. Namely to help; to heal. To set people free when they are stuck.

This matters because there are reportedly more women then men now qualified in the US and UK as hypnotherapists (as far as anyone can tell, given the plethora of professional bodies). However, the traditional power dynamic of hypnosis – powerful man, weaker woman – is incredibly persistent. (Has anything moved on since ditzy Eve and the sneaky snake in the Garden of Eden?) It's rather a shame that the whole thing is overshadowed by those powerful tropes, when all you need is to visit your local

The hypnotist works his dark arts on an innocent female, in 1891. (Think of *Macbeth*: 'Her eyes are open, but their sense is shut.')

"A FEW PASSES, MADE IN THE USUAL WAY, SUFFICED" (p. 371).

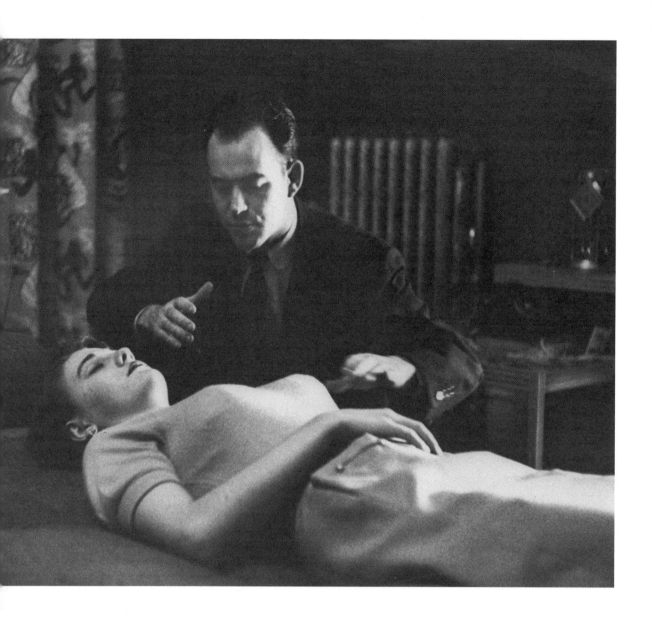

This image from 1956, a photograph from *Life* magazine, updates the essential elements of the dark, intense, powerful man and the susceptible woman dressed in light colours … by the addition of a push-up bra.

hypnotherapist so you can deliver the best man's speech at your brother's wedding. This is a typical transaction, happening right now on a high street near you – not that you'd know it from the media. Meanwhile there is a stare of female stage hypnotists (note collective noun, please!) currently performing, but they always seem to be billed as 'female stage hypnotist' – i.e. an

exception, deviating from the powerful cliché that is known to sell. When their gender becomes unexceptional, then something will have changed. And as I keep hinting – the world of hypnosis is ripe for change. (I think it's very exciting!)

Right now, I need to introduce you to some extraordinary women: hypnotists and pioneers. The exceptions that prove the rule.

Annie De Montford (1836–1882)

I'd like to introduce you to Annie De Montford: she was a mesmerist. Not a lady mesmerist; a mesmerist. This alone is enough to command our respect. She was also called a psychological star, and an electrobiologist, and occasionally a hypnotist but more often than not she called herself a mesmerist. Her billing claimed that her 'mind governs the world' and that she was the 'wonder of the age'. It therefore seems strange that she slipped into historical oblivion.

I discovered her in the British Library when I was researching there, and was intrigued by the ups and downs of her career. She was born Annie Riley in Leicestershire in 1836 and her father was a mill-worker. By 1861, she was staying with William Henry Chadwick, who had been one of the Chartists – the famous working class political agitators who demanded political reform in the 1840s. He is described in the census of 1861 as a 'Lecturer on Magnetism', and Annie is described as a 'Lecturer on Phrenology'. So she'd clearly fallen in with an interesting crowd, and she had soon taken the name of the big hall in the area where she was

born, De Montford, and started practising as a mesmerist. There are lots of mentions of her in the trade publication for performers, *The Era*, and between 1871 and 1882 she seems to have been working constantly. There is a detailed description of her performance in a local newspaper of the time, which reveals that what she was doing in the 1870s and what still happens in stage hypnotism acts now is remarkably similar.

They seemed very impressed by the fact that she was a lady – though De Montford didn't make a feature of this on her posters. Less impressed was the *Dundee Courier and Argus* in 1875, which carried a story about Annie being exposed in America as an imposter.

An investigation by an American reporter revealed that she had been caught using stooges, who she employed, and that certain audience members had become obsessed with her and volunteered to be her subjects night after night. Obviously there was a high degree

This is Jean-Martin Charcot demonstrating hypnosis on a patient at Salpêtrière, called Blanche. Poor Blanche. Healed? Well possibly. But by the full force of the patriarchy. There are two things going on here: hypnosis and the sexualised subjugation of women. It's important that we recognise them as two distinct things, because for many years they have been intertwined.

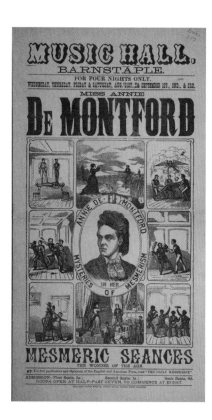

We have the stage magician Henry Evans who performed under the name Evanion to thank for these posters of Annie. He collected them – along with thousands of other items. They were bought by the British Library in 1895.

of showpersonship in Annie's act. One of the reasons I love hypnosis is that fine line between science and showbiz, and clearly here she crossed that line. But whether she crossed the line between showbiz and out-and-out fraud is not clear. Crucially the exposé in the Dundee newspaper seems to have failed to ruin her career, and she carried on touring the UK until 1882.

Was that it? She worked, experienced success, then got ill and didn't work any more. Is it that simple? Apparently, yes. She died on 12 October 1882. From looking at her death certificate I wonder what was the 'supposed injury' that gave her jaundice and liver failure. She was only 46. Perhaps I'm sentimental about her, but she was 'the most powerful mesmerist in the world' … and then she wasn't.

So I'm glad to be celebrating her. She was a trailblazer who teetered on the edge of legality and respectability, but she must have believed in it. Her connection to the Chartists suggests she was in the game to help people, rather than being a showy charlatan. I imagine all the touring was hard work, and maybe some nights she didn't feel like claiming that her 'mind ruled the world', but she probably went ahead and performed anyway. So I'm happy to have restored her legacy a little and to have written a song about her. 'No end of laughter', reads her bill matter. Well – that was always going to be an exaggeration – there is always going to be an end to laughter, but it's good to reflect, while looking at this theatrical ephemera, on the ephemeral nature of life itself.

OXFORD HALL, ILFRACOMBE.

MIND GOVERNS THE WORLD.

MISS ANNIE DE MONTFORD

THE PSYCHOLOGICAL STAR

FOR TWO NIGHTS ONLY,
MONDAY & TUESDAY, AUGUST 29 & 30.

The Little Hypnotic Sunbeam

Mrs. Herbert L. FLINT

Mrs Flint

Let's take a brief detour to the world of Mrs Flint. Now I'm sadly illustrating the parlous state of the history of women in hypnosis by including a woman known only by her husband's first name, in that weird way beloved only by minor aristocracy and the flower rotas of church magazines. Mrs Herbert L. Flint performed with her husband in America from the late-nineteenth century onwards. They were managed by Thomas F. Adkin, who had a small stable of stage hypnotists (including the author of our favourite correspondence course, by the man named by the god of names, Xenophon LaMotte Sage).

Little is known of Mrs Flint, except that she and her husband seemed to be blessed with great graphic designers. Their posters pop up all the time when researching the history of the subject, and rightly so. Allowing herself to be called 'The little hypnotic sunbeam' doesn't earn her any more kudos in the context of this chapter, but surely all can be forgiven for the partial credit she must take for Flint's Hypnotic Skirt Dance. This transvestite manifestation of sheer perverted *joie de*

vivre raises more questions than the image could ever answer, not least of which is what is going on with Jesus. He obviously has very flouncy robes and very long arms, which is fair enough, but why is he presiding over this scene of what could only be – for the period of the tour in Middle America – a vision of nothing more than the heralding of total social and moral disintegration? The feminist in me notes that Mrs Flint is the only one smiling on this poster; not the men in frocks, not Jesus and certainly not her husband. Maybe she was more powerful than history can tell us for certain. Or maybe Jesus just wanted her for a 'hypnotic sunbeam'. We will never know.

Joan Brandon (1914–1979)

I can't tell you how revolutionary these images are (though perhaps you are beginning to get a sense of it). The older, powerful woman hypnotising the younger, passive man turns the iconography of the practice since its early days completely on its head. Sadly, these images of Joan Brandon are complete aberrations, and they would still be revolutionary in the mainstream media now.

Of course Joan had to revisit the classic 'human plank or bridge', using a male subject and inviting a friend in polka dots and worryingly high heels to help her out. This is, of course, nothing to do with hypnosis. As we discovered earlier, if the subject is correctly positioned the human body can stand much more weight than looks possible from the perspective of the audience. Though it is possible her subject might have needed to be hypnotised to stand a stiletto in the underpants department. I can't get enough of the human bridge, so here are a couple more examples before I tell you more about Joan.

Joan Brandon started as a dancer, then progressed to doing sophisticated magic. A 'blonde stunner' who could do a mean dancing cane act, she billed herself as a stage magician all through the 1940s. In 1953 she transitioned to describing herself as a stage hypnotist. She published a bestselling book in 1956 and was the darling of the press for a short while, riding out the 1950s fascination with hypnotism. This was slightly confused because it was in part sparked by the Bridey Murphy story. But that doesn't seem to have bothered Joan. She made a good career for herself in the late 50s and into the 60s. Her last public performance

was in 1970 at the Mountain Park Resort, which has the slightly depressing slogan 'More fun for less'; it doesn't sound very classy. Poor Joan. (But I'm being sentimental again, and perhaps faintly patronising. It's probably deeply ingrained sexism just like that I'm accusing generations of hypnotists of – though I hope not.) I just admire her for getting an act together – being the only woman doing it – and slogging around making the act work, while putting on what looks like a damn fine show and writing a book that even today, if you

were wanting to learn stage hypnotism, would be a good place to start your study. Let's hope more women, and in fact anyone who isn't a bloke in a slightly sweaty suit, decide to do just that. The next generation, I challenge you to live up to the legacy of Annie and Joan.

The older, powerful woman hypnotising the younger, passive man turns the iconography of the practice since its early days completely on its head.

MY STORY

PART THREE

All right, back to me. It's 2012. If you remember, I was now clutching a diploma in cognitive behavioural hypnotherapy, and could do a stage hypnotism routine.

I had invented a character called Derek Diamond ('formally known as Baz Vegas – but the case was never proved and the kiddy didn't die'). He was the owner of a working men's club called The Razzle, and was a former cruise-ship entertainer. He did a very standard 45-minute stage hypnotism routine, involving volunteers from the audience who ended up singing like pop stars, dancing like ballerinas and then claiming they didn't know what they'd been doing when it was all over.

It was all good fun, especially when it worked as the centrepiece to my experiential theatre show, which brought The Razzle club to life. However, it was not really what I wanted to be doing with hypnosis. It's a laugh, but it takes from the participants. As a performer, I was to encouraging them to give. Derek's act was slightly – or even downright – exploitative. It was a cheap sugar hit when I wanted to be offering a sustaining low-GI meal.

The British Library invited me to be their first ever Artist in Residence. They asked me what I wanted to study and I, of course, said hypnosis. (I'm a bit one-track. I'm fascinated by hypnosis, OK? To quote Bette Midler: 'Do they dump on the Pope 'cos all he talks about is God?') So I spent a year at the library researching the history of the subject. *My* history, that made sense to me – not the history that had filtered down through popular culture, or the scientific angle that I'd studied for my hypnotherapy training. I spent a long time thinking creatively about what hypnosis could give me theatrically that conventional performance couldn't. I gradually picked away until I came to the conclusion that I wanted to present the thought that 'change can happen'. We often feel stuck, and I wanted to stand on stage and invite low-level role-play that asked one question: 'How would it be if …?' How would it be if, for example, we all were happy; how would it be if we were all the audience at a music hall performance in 1900; how would it be

This is stage hypnotist
Derek Diamond in
action – blond wig,
sequined jacket, slash
curtain. Classy.

How would it be if we were all free from worry, if we were all less fearful, if we were all as free as we have always wanted to be?

if we were all free from worry, if we were all less fearful, if we were all as free as we have always wanted to be?

Don't shoot me for being a hippy. There's a long history of this inclination in hypnosis, from Avicenna (980–1037; a Persian psychologist and physician) onwards. I was inspired by many people, including unlikely sources such as Henry Blythe and Paul McKenna, who want to use their stage skills to effect personal change. They are my heroes of hypnosis. I am most fascinated by people who started as hypnotists and then developed into becoming healers. This is most likely because I hope to make the same journey. This is certainly the journey the audience witnesses in the Singing Hypnotist show. So a special shout-out to all of those people, from Dr Vint and Annie De Montford, through Joan Brandon and society hypnotherapist Max Kirsten to Gil Boyne. There are many more, but I find these people's stories most moving and straightforward. What are we here for, after all, if not to 'alleviate the suffering of [our] fellow creatures', as Dr Vint put it. So much popular entertainment encourages stasis. The audience leave unchanged: entertained, yes, but changed, no. But why not entertain while also presenting simple ideas that suggest how easy it is to break habits? They are just habits, after all. They might feel like us, but they are not us.

And then also, I wanted to sing. Throughout my research I had always assumed, somewhere in the midsts of time, I would find a hypnotist who sang. It seems the obvious meeting point between entertainment and science – but I never did find that person. So I invented him: the Singing Hypnotist. I started writing a character, set in the late-nineteenth century. I wrote him several songs, a back story and a stage routine, and I performed him several times at the British Library. Then I realised that he wasn't a character – he was me. I was him. That might not strike you as a devastatingly complex realisation, but for a character comedian it was pretty challenging.

So now the Singing Hypnotist takes his audience through a series of tricks, experiments and wonders, all presented through song. There are many songs and several mood swings in the show, but the central part is a sung-through ten-minute section, taking volunteers from the audience from induction through deepeners, into hypnosis, suggestions with tests that the audience can witness, and post-hypnotic suggestions – and ends with the volunteers being brought out of trance. It's basically me talking about how our brains work, but in a very experiential way. After all, the one thing we all share is our experience of consciousness. It's the filter through which everything happens, and yet we are seldom aware of it. We talk about it with each other even less. I don't want to get technical on stage about neural pathways, because we know what consciousness feels like, even if we don't know the scientific terms to describe it. We are less familiar with the notion that our way of thinking is easy to change. It's a strange part of being alive that our minds feel set and slightly stuck somehow.

So the show says 'change can happen'.

We are less familiar with the notion that our way of thinking is easy to change. It's a strange part of being alive that our minds feel set and slightly stuck somehow.

But who effects the change? (A-ha!) So really, the show is about power: hypnotism is all about power. Little fellas becoming the Wizard of Oz. I ask my audience whether they want me to be powerful enough to effect change in their lives. The show then gently progresses until I finally ask the question, 'Why do you want to give up your power to somebody else?' I then say, 'How would it be if you were already powerful enough yourself?' It's the ultimate DIY show. After proving that they do have power by getting them to hypnotise me, we then celebrate by singing and dancing together. It's silly and it's trivial, and it does involve more ill-advised synchronised dance routines than strictly necessary, but it makes a profound truth that we are the ones in control of our lives. Hypnosis is just a tool. You could call it self-hypnosis, self-confidence, delusion, prayer or determination.

So that's the Singing Hypnotist. He is all-powerful, his mind rules the world, he can sing the change your life needs, he can control your destiny. But you know what? Tell him to get lost. You can do it better yourself.

HEROES OF HYPNOSIS

Avicenna (980–1037)

I love this ancient Persian thinker – Avicenna was a trailblazer. He identified hypnosis and called it *al-Wahm al-Amil* in Arabic, which sounds great and is often translated as 'pleasant, dreamy imagination'. Who wouldn't want that in their life on a regular basis? His great contribution was to distinguish between trance and sleep. He connected words to feelings, and feelings to illnesses. A man ahead of his time.

Henry Blythe

Henry Blythe was a stage hypnotist who crossed over the great divide into healing, which he called 'curative hypnosis'. He is an obscure figure in the history of hypnosis, but one I like very much indeed. That stems mainly from his wonderful book, *The Truth About Hypnotism* (1971), which is unintentionally hilarious in authorial style and content, but also very moving for some unexpected reason. It's a great mixture of fascinating theory, showbiz anecdotes and very slightly purple (sort of wisteria) prose. Favourite chapters include '1969 The Year of the Warts', and 'The Twilight Zone', which deals with his attempts to cure homosexuality and other 'sex perversions'. He is benign about this (trust me). He seems genuinely conflicted about whether homosexuality could and indeed should

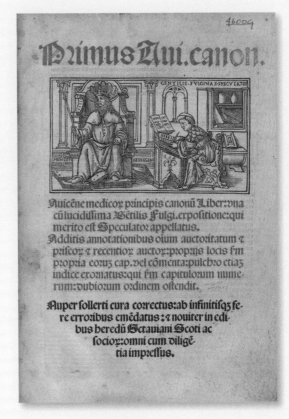

be eradicated, and ahead of his time in his compassion. He is also charming, humble – and at the same time an incorrigible self-promoter. He stood for parliament as the Labour candidate for Gloucester with the slogan 'Look into my Eyes and Vote for Me'.

Other stunts included hypnotising the entire Gloucester City FC team to improve their performance. Online you can find a feature by Pathé News from 1959 about his attempt. It's called 'Svengali

Means Goals', and it ends with the commentary: 'They won that match. The next, when Henry was away, they lost. That speaks for itself!' At the time this would have been thought of as harmless fun, but now hypnosis in sports science is big business.

He pops up again in 1960 with a bizarre stunt to hypnotise learner drivers to enable them to pass their driving test. He is pictured with his daughter Sally who later went on to fail her test, as the local newspaper reported with glee.

Unlike Blythe's work in sports hypnotism, his pioneering work in hypnotising drivers didn't catch on.

Henry Blythe has had a bizarre afterlife, and is currently running his own Facebook page promoting his hypnosis records. This is run by someone who became slightly obsessed with Blythe after hearing his *Stop Smoking* album (in which Henry very kindly suggests that you might like to think about stopping this filthy habit if it's all the same to you). It's billed on YouTube as 'Worst Hypnotist Ever??' which is a bit harsh, but you sort of know what they mean. Blythe's catchphrase was 'Grip and glare'. I suggest you look it up – you'll be glad you did.

His son, Peter Huxley-Blythe, had a distinguished Navy career and wrote books about war, but seems to have come round to his father's way of thinking later, as he founded the Blythe

College of Hypnosis and Psychotherapy in the late 1960s. It's still going, as the National College of Hypnosis and Psychotherapy. So good old Henry has had a lasting impact on the important use of hypnosis as a therapeutic tool, and I suspect that would have pleased him, as it does me.

I am unsure why Mr Blythe delights me so much. I would attempt a reference to his blythe spirit, but I am not him, and wouldn't be able to pull off such flowery prose. So why does he matter? Well, despite being kitsch, slightly foolish and a bit of a duffer, he is wonderfully genuine in his aims to effect positive transformations in people's lives. For me, he sums up the wonderful range of this subject: I salute him.

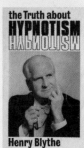

Opposite: Thank goodness Mr Blythe cleared the road of traffic before trying this experiment.

Top: Here are Henry and Sally before getting into the car.

HYPNOTIC PATENTS

Here is a photograph from the Toronto Star from March 1966, showing Ralph Albert and his son Joe looking at some of the equipment he uses in his hypnosis experiments. Apparently they are a hypnodisc, flash-beat metronome and a brainwave synchroniser. No mention is made of the fact that they are being displayed on a novelty African bar in the corner of Ralph's sitting room. And those wall lamps are a worry. (Focus on the hypnotic equipment!) Hypnosis is a pretty simple thing to induce. But that hasn't stopped people like Ralph from making it seem complex. I hope Joe made it out of that house OK and is happy.

A great deal of this book consists of my uncovering of the glorious, tortuous and convoluted ways that people who know about hypnosis have used to make it seem as complicated as possible. This isn't sinister; it's human nature. We like complexity. We like to argue about it from the position that our complex view is the right one. We like the fact that *we* understand something, but it's dangerous when used by those stupider than us.

Fig. 12.—Group of eight persons under the influence of a rotatory mirror apparatus (after Luys).

Hang on for a moment – this thought will continue – but first I have to sing a hymn of praise to patents…..

Ahh the Patents! You know how it's socially acceptable – even culturally essential – to spend days and days watching box sets of "important" US drama. I don't do that. But I have several times taken myself off to the British Library to wade through files and files. And people think I'm the odd one! Would you rather passively absorb hours of made up people in made up places having a terrible time, whilst you neglect to wash or communicate with the outside world. Or would you, like me, rather read of the glories and the follies of human invention. The desire, the hope, the hairs-breadth whisper of possibility just out of reach. It's the most entertainment you can have for free in a public place. There are x rated patents for filthy inventions. There are stupid inventions that take your breath away. There's various ones to enable you to do a wee in public without anyone noticing. Many from the prudish midst of time are devices to prevent masturbation. Many in recent times are devices to aid masturbation. That tells you all you need

to know about social and sexual history in the last 100 years or so. All human life is there. My next book is going to be all about the Patents. Seriously. Looking through these files tells you all you need to know about human beings, their worries, their desires and the Heath-Robinson-esque solutions they have come up with to alleviate and attain them. Ahh Patents Office! You are the navigation of the river of human existence. I love your precision, you order, your archaic filing system, I love a dog-carrying device involving a muzzle and an anal probe, I love patents.

Thanks for bearing with me. That had to be done. One more point though. The pronunciation of patent is a little troublesome. When you're referring to the legal protection of an invention, which we are, then it's pronounced "Pat-uhnt". If you're English then for all other uses of the word it's "pay-tuhnt". If you're American then you say "Pat-uhnt" for everything, except when something is obvious, when you say "Pay-tuhnt". I hope that's helpful, not patronising, and not "Paytuhnt"ly obvious.

E.A. Hart – *Hypnotism and the New Witchcraft*, 1891

Over the years there have been many applications for devices to help you get hypnotised. The early ones were apparently often detailed to help with inducing sleep, or as cures for insomnia – the theory being that many more people would want help with insomnia than would want an expensive piece of machinery that could hypnotise them. But what they are really attempting to do is induce a state of self-hypnosis that in turn induces sleep. All of which you could do for yourself without the machine at all, but let's not be a spoilsport. One of the best of these devices also happens to be the oldest on record.

Patent [2]

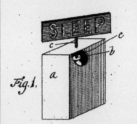

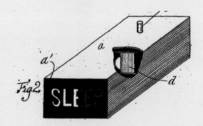

This machine from August 1899 has two mechanisms whereby the word 'SLEEP' ('or any other such word or phrase containing the necessary suggestion') is revealed. One turns slowly while the other gradually lights up, and this is done with a mirror. It's beautifully elegant and simple, in theory. Except that it's not – it's incredibly complicated, and all it does is make your eyes tired while you stare for too long at a one-word suggestion. Wonderful. I don't think many were made.

Patent [1]

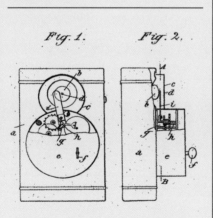

This one is from 1913, and represents the French attempting to get the UK patent for 'an apparatus for inducing hypnotic sleep by the intermittent appearance of a light'. I'm sure it was lovely.

Patent [3]

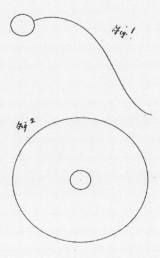

We are now in 1909, and Haydn Brown from Surrey certainly couldn't be accused of over-complexity. His 'invention' consists of a 'bright spherical or globular or other shaped object attached to the end of either a stiff-curved or soft-flexible wire rod or jointed folding or telescopic shaft. In other words, it's a ball on a wire. You attach it to a chair or a bedstead and stare at it to obtain hypnotic or natural sleep. (Wow. He went to the bother of patenting that? He must have spent hours sketching and writing. It's a ball on a wire, Haydn!) And if you want to induce sleep or a trance by eye fixation, you can encourage your patient or yourself to stare at any fixed point on the ceiling. And yet, it's all there: his hopes of being a leader in the field of hypnotic sleep induction, curing insomnia and making a few quid. And immortality. Which, thanks to the Patent Office, he has achieved.

Patent [4]

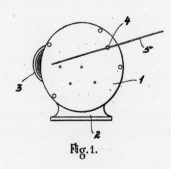

Fig.1.

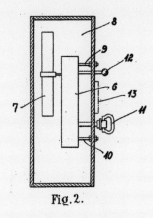

Fig.2.

In the 1920s a German doctor made this. 'It is a well known fact that the uniform noise of a travelling railway train has a soporific effect.' This brilliant little machine, with its space-age futuristic, design replicates that by producing a wearying low humming noise. I'm not an expert on low frequencies, but I thought they could be unsettling and made people go a bit bonkers. If you fancy making yourselves one of these and reporting back, do please let me know.

Patent [5]

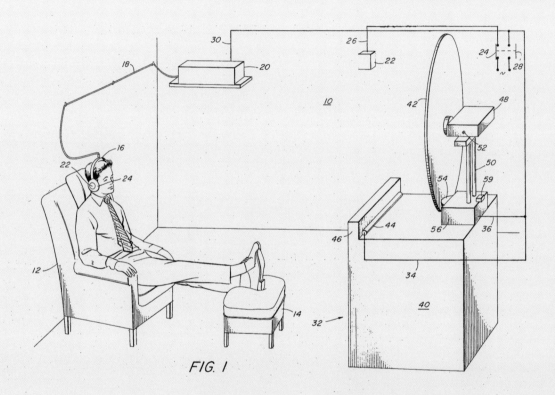

FIG. 1

I give this one (from the US in the 1970s) a huge metaphorical round of applause for its thoroughness. It's not merely an invention; it's a whole room. It's an entire room full of gadgetry to induce hypnosis. (Wow – that's a lot of bother.) You could ask someone to read a script to bring about hypnosis. You could do it for yourself. Or, you could move house, get a spare room, install Mr Paul King's devices and as quickly and easily as that, pop yourself off into a hypnotic trance. There is nothing I don't love about this illustration. The man is beautifully dressed, extremely handsome and very happy with his hypnotic state. The detail is so precise, and the accompanying notes make your head bleed with their pedantry.

Patent [6]

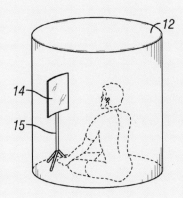

Let it not be said that, as we approach the present, mankind is losing any sense of scale or ambition in the bonkers hypnotic devices field. This one was first registered in 2010; you could probably buy one if you wanted. They might of course be used in laboratories all over the world, in which case my irreverence is extremely misplaced. But I sincerely do love this. It's a new-age tube that you sit in to meditate and get hypnotised. The fact that people have been doing this for millennia using only a cushion seems irrelevant when you look at the sheer bravado of the complexity laid out for us in this diagram. Which, when it comes down to it, seems to me to depict little more than someone meditating into a mirror. (I think I would personally go for the options outlined in Fig. 6, which have the luxury addition of air openings 'thereby making the environment within the structure more comfortable for the person' ... which is patentese for 'making it possible to breathe'.

I salute all the inventors. No doubt there are many more like this in the Intellectual Property Office. Next time you pull a sick day, leave your duvet behind and go and browse through the weird and wonderful applications in the British Library or the US Patent and Trademark Office. (Or wait until my book about it comes out.) These patents belong to us all. The inventions may save our lives, or they may be ridiculous, but their inventors went through an awful lot so that you didn't have to. They are a mark of a civilised society.

Oh go on then. I can't resist. Here's a machine for kicking yourself up the arse:

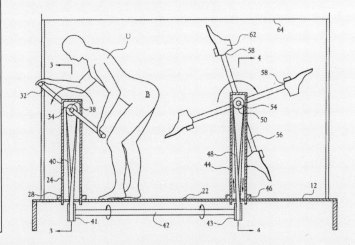

ALAN MITCHELL

HARLEY STREET HYPNOTIST

FOUR SQUARE BOOKS

2/6

Pollack

This is one of my favourite clinical hypnotherapy books. How the author approved the cover is a mystery, because the salacious imagery is completely at odds with the serious tone of the book itself. I wouldn't wish it any other way, though, because the naive painting – with its busty lady, odd arrangement of figures and bewildering hypnotic spiral – absolutely nails the notion of the hypnotist as a sexy, slightly dangerous, powerful figure, probably in a stylish mac. A kind of therapeutic James Bond. I imagine many a bored housewife went to see Alan in Harley Street in the 1960s expecting a walk on the wild side, and found themselves having a toasted teacake in John Lewis 90 minutes later, no longer afraid of dogs but mildly disappointed they hadn't been lightly abused and whisked off to the Riviera.

WHAT ABOUT ME?

I t's all very well delving thousands of years into the antecedents of hypnosis, and digging out obscure books from the bowels of libraries, but by this point you would have every right to be shouting loudly inside your own head, 'Yes, yes ... but what about me?'

'What can it do for me? I am a smorgasbord of minor frailties, fallibilities and faults. I'm mildly interested in looking at fat fellas with luxuriant moustaches, but what I really want to ask is ... can hypnosis help me?'

Looking at the wealth of material featured in this book, going back hundreds of years, I am amazed that there is still a fundamental misunderstanding about hypnosis: that it is something that is done to you; a mysterious process for which you must give up your free will. In reality it is a process that you inculcate in yourself. Your first experiences of it might be as a recipient, from a trained practitioner, but ultimately it's a muscle that you strengthen over time. It's experiential. A helpful, pleasant, altered form of ordinary consciousness that, once you can access it, you can go to whenever you want. If you study the history of the subject for yourself, you'll see too that this point is

made repeatedly, but it gets lost in the seductive glamour of stage hypnotism, and in the unintelligent tropes you will find in popular culture.

So yes, hypnosis really can help you, as one of a range of techniques to help keep you on the rails. I would say that the best approach is to start off with professional

If you're expecting to be able to control people using nefarious means like this one, you're barking up the wrong tree. Hypnosis is most useful as one of a range of tools for getting through life slightly more smoothly – not a fast track to world domination. This is reality, people, not a kids' cartoon.

A—CENTRAL GAZE
B—ORDINARY GAZE

A HARD INTERVIEW MADE EASY BY A KNOWLEDGE OF THE LAWS OF MENTAL CURRENTS.

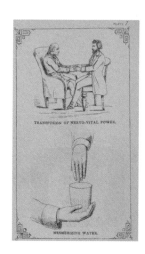

'Evidence' of the treatment of a huge range of ailments. No word on efficacy, and none of these would be treated by a hypnotherapist now. But like this one, clinical hypnotherapists' websites often have a long list of issues they can help with. Usually most of them could be bracketed under the heading of 'anxiety management'.

help, and then skill yourself up so that self-hypnosis is an option to turn to whenever you need it. I'll assume that's the case, so we'll look at clinical hypnotherapy to begin with, then self-hypnosis later.

But first, put aside the thought that you can't be hypnotised. It's a strangely self-limiting notion, but lots of people think they won't be susceptible. I am sure that's something to do with the fact that a lot of us feel 'stuck', and it's at the root of our unhappiness; a heaviness that is the exact opposite of the light, energetic feeling that comes with easy change. And easy change is absolutely possible. I love the standard answer you get from hypnotherapists about who can be hypnotised: 'Anyone who is creative, intelligent and playful is a good candidate.' That answer is of course designed to flatter, encourage and reassure people, but it has the added bonus of being true. So let's celebrate being creative, intelligent and playful, and forget feeling stuck! Anyway, the answer is, yes you can be hypnotised. So how are you going to go about it?

It's all about empowering yourself. You could spend the rest of your life looking for someone to deliver results with your

issue and then teach you how to manage it yourself. It's like going to a hairstylist for a new look that means you never have to visit one ever again.

You'll find hypnotists claiming great results with an enormous range of problems, but broadly speaking hypnotherapy is most effective when dealing with anything relating to anxiety. Nailing that helps with a lot of aspects of life, from stopping smoking, to being able to deliver a presentation, to standing up to your nasty boss, to not being afraid of buttons on a clown's jacket. It's also very effective at helping with pain management. Anxiety management is also at the heart of hypno-birthing.

Like everything in life these days, from going on holiday to plastic surgery, its all about the correct online research. This can be somewhat exhausting, but incredibly liberating.

Every high street has a clinical hypnotherapist these days; an internet search will probably bring you a range of options not far from your home. It's sustaining a lot of careers – so it must work, right? Well, yes is the answer but that doesn't mean that choosing the right one is easy. Hypnosis is a really safe treatment, so the biggest issue you are likely to face is a sheer waste of time rather than serious psychological harm, but still it pays to do some research.

The fact that astounds most people is that UK laws don't dictate how much training you have to have before you are allowed to practise as a hypnotherapist. Anyone can set themselves up in business. (Oh crikey!) So do check what qualifications your therapist has got, and follow that up by checking for membership of a professional body. There are lots of these, but they are united by umbrella organisations such as the UK Confederation of Hypnotherapy Organisations and the American Association of Professional Hypnotherapists. All therapists should tell you what indemnity insurance they have. If they don't mention it, then ask.

Fees range hugely for treatment, but remember – with a hypnotherapist you will only need on average a couple of sessions (in this way it differs from psychotherapy, which is more of a long-term relationship). Maybe one, maybe four, but that's extreme. So you can probably afford not to go for the cheapest

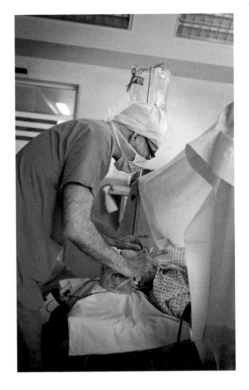

Hypnosis for surgery. Apart from the small number of people who are allergic to anaesthetic, hardly any of us are going to have surgery using only hypnosis. I think if science has gone to the bother of inventing an effective way to be rendered delightfully unconscious without side-effects then it's rude not to use it, but we can all use basic self-hypnosis techniques every time we go to the dentist or have injections or minor procedures. Self-hypnosis is awesomely powerful, so why not take advantage?

option – in fact, I would recommend *not* going for the cheapest. A mid-range price shows confidence. (Being really expensive probably just means they draw their clients exclusively from the pool of oil oligarchs' mistresses, and good luck to them.)

Ring, and ask to talk to the therapist on the phone. Ask them what experience they have of working with the issue that is concerning you. If they sound vague or admit to being a little unsure, then find someone who isn't. It's always good if they have an assistant – it shows they are busy. (But then again, it might just show they are

---

Hypnosis is a really safe treatment, so the biggest issue you are likely to face is a sheer waste of time rather than serious psychological harm, but still it pays to do some research.

There's nothing mystical or magical going on. You're paying for skills, not sacrificing a goat or hanging out with a latter-day Madame Arcati. You should expect straightforward, professional, clear communication.

good at doing accents and pretending to put you through ...) Trust your intuition. When you do arrive at their rooms, again trust your instincts. If it doesn't feel professional then you can always walk away. Remember you are there to get help, advice and tutoring on how to manage your relationship with your own consciousness. There's nothing mystical or magical going on. You're paying for skills, not sacrificing a goat or hanging out with a latter-day Madame Arcati. You should expect straightforward, professional, clear communication.

I personally wouldn't worry too much about the type of hypnosis they offer. The techniques differ slightly, and it really makes sense to combine hypnotherapy with NLP or CBT (cognitive behavioural therapy), but they should, broadly speaking, be similar in approach. Hypnotherapists are like any gang – they love to argue about different terms, ideas and approaches. It's human nature. People who make conservatories probably get very exercised by different double-glazing techniques. We just want glass that doesn't leak. This is probably most relevant in the hypnotherapy world when it comes to the 'state' theory. Much

of the history of hypnosis has consisted of arguments about the state versus the non-state theory of hypnosis. I suggest we forget all about this, and focus on the fact that it has been proved over and over again to be really good at getting you out of being in a state – as in 'a right state'. So keep focused on what you're asking for help with, and let the therapists go to their conferences to argue about techniques and technicalities.

Isn't the worst part of any professional consultation when they give you homework? That moment when you realise that there is no magic cure ... there is no all powerful Wizard of Oz figure who will make everything all right. You will continue to be you, just with one minor concern dealt with – but only if you put in the effort at home. Well, yes, I'm here to tell you that hypnotherapy is just like that. A good therapist will give you the skills for you to develop in your own time. It's not magic. (Nothing is magic, except Magic. And that just tricks.) We know this, because we are grown-ups, but sometimes we refuse to believe it.

So do your homework, and change will come. That's not the stuff of miracles –

but it's the stuff of profound, exciting real life.

Very conscientious readers might remember that I didn't start hypnosis with a visit to a professional. I just downloaded an MP3 from the internet. There is a huge range to choose from – good, bad and very indifferent – and I think I was lucky, but I wouldn't warn anyone off this option. Go straight for being independent if you're that kind of person. It's certainly cheaper, and you can always ask for professional advice later on. You'll end up on your own with your consciousness sooner or later anyway, so maybe it's best that you, your conscious mind and your subconscious mind all get the love-in started sooner rather than later.

Have a good search on the internet. Use your intuition. You know a lot about hypnosis now, so you'll get a good sense from a quick listen as to whether or not something is for you. I would say that it makes sense to engage with a hypnotherapist who has a good strong practice; you are then simply choosing to engage with them via their online offering rather than schlepping to their consulting rooms. Get to know them and their voice, and then you can use a range of their downloads or apps. An app simply consolidates an audio session, other suggestions and advice in a fancy, easy-to-access way. This is especially useful for issues that benefit from regular topping up, like weight management or smoking cessation.

The biggest question, which it's important to address however you choose to access hypnosis, is how to manage your expectations of what it will feel like. Any good hypnotherapist will deal with this before they start counting backwards from 100. As we know, media representations have misled us since we started watching kids' cartoons. So you should know that you will not become a googly-eyed loon. You will not be unconscious. You will always feel like you. You will not be in ecstasy or in agony. You will be you. And that will be enough to effect profound change. In fact, acknowledging the rightness of simply being you is the start of the process. Forget all the images in this glossy, attractive book – they are all wrong. Get up, find a mirror, look at yourself, close your eyes and relax. That's what a hypnotised person looks like. Oh – yes – there's a slight flaw in my instructions, but you get the idea.

SELF-HYPNOSIS

You'll have worked out by now that, while I have the utmost respect for hypnotists, therapists and scientists who use hypnosis to study our brains, I ultimately believe in DIY; I think it's the way forward. Make the hypnotist redundant! And in the spirit of teaching a man to fish, I am about to encourage you to make mongers of the world redundant, and help yourself to heal.

The last chapter looked at getting treatment for yourself, and I would certainly recommend that for a whole range of problems. But always remember the basic message of this book. The history of this subject is littered with people who have a vested interest in making you believe that hypnosis is complex, mysterious and beyond your ken. It is not beyond your ken. It is your ken. It literally *is* your knowledge and experience of how your own consciousness works. Hypnosis is simply doing a little relationship therapy between your conscious mind and your unconscious mind. They've got into slightly lazy bad habits, but ultimately they love each other. You just need to reconnect them. You could get a hypnotist to do that for you, or you could do it for yourself.

Self-hypnosis has changed my life; changed my relationship with myself.

It was a revelation to contemplate that I might treat myself with compassion, dignity and gentleness. This is the basis of mental health.

I think that contrary to what we normally believe, it's not the nutters who talk to themselves. Instead it's the sensible ones, the ones with a good relationship with themselves. I call it having a word with yourself. You might call it self-care. It's properly parenting yourself. The voice that gently suggests you might not need the entire packet of chocolate biscuits, or that it might be a good idea to take yourself off to bed before you get overtired and weepy. Self-hypnosis is just a technique to get good at this.

So I have three practical exercises for you, and the first two aren't really hypnosis at all. The first is mindfulness. The second is meditation. Then the third is self-hypnosis.

This is a lady hypnotising herself using a record made by a hypnotist and staring at a pair of eyes. (It's all a bit *Big Brother*.) But don't let this put you off self-hypnosis – it's actually much simpler than this!

When I was a child I used to hate books with practical bits in them. I would always skip those bits, never again to return to 'making a present for your granny from washing-up liquid bottles'. If you are about to do the same now, I would urge you to think again. Consciousness is the ultimate experiential activity. We can only experience it by having our attention drawn to experiencing it. So come on, kids … let's experience it.

Exercise 1

You need yourself, a chair and a timer on your phone or stopwatch.

Take yourself to a quiet place. Reassure yourself that nothing weird is happening. This is not the occult. You are not joining a cult. You're simply going to sit quietly for a few minutes.

Sit upright on a chair. Lying down is always nice, but it does send the signal to our brain that it's time for a snooze, as does leaning back in the chair. Sit upright, with your spine doing the job of supporting you. Be aware of yourself sitting on the chair; be aware of the noise in the room, and outside the room. Become aware of your position in the world. Become aware of simply being. Now set a timer for three minutes. Don't close your eyes. Simply see what comes up for you in that short period of time. Don't do any fancy breathing or thinking. You are. That's it. When the timer goes off, congratulate yourself. You've just practised mindfulness.

Now I'm pretty sure that you will want to go off and research mindfulness. There are many courses and guides available, and it's life-changing stuff. But before you do that, try …

Exercise 2

You need exactly the same things. And in fact you are going to do exactly the same as before, but this time with an added focus on observing your thoughts. Observing. Not controlling. Not changing. Observing. When you catch yourself thinking, you simply say 'thinking' to yourself. You then return to sitting quietly and being aware of your breathing. Your brain will start to get very busy, offering you many useful thoughts, bits of information, perhaps even songs. You simply say 'thinking', smiling with compassion at how eager and productive your brain is before becoming aware of your breathing again.

Start with three minutes, then you can build up to as long as you want – although I find my legs complain loudly after around an hour. But that's meditation. It's nothing complex; it's simple and it's easy. You can spend the rest of your life practising it and never master it, but at heart it's simple and it's easy.

Again, this can lead you off into an orgy of googling and researching. There are many things you can do with this basic instruction, but both of these techniques are a good build-up to hypnotising yourself, which I outline in …

Exercise 3

You will need a recording device – many smartphones do this really easily. However you do it, you just need to be able to record yourself and then listen back to yourself.

Hypnosis is a trick to distract the conscious mind – this is the protective bit that worries about keeping you safe, keeping you fed and warm and whether you should have a wee before you get on the bus. Listening to an authoritative voice speaking directly to your subconscious allows the conscious mind to relax a little; to give up control. To give control, in fact, to this cocky person who seems to know what he's doing. But what if that cocky person was you?

I love this technique. It might seem a little cringey to you at first – like a form of self-help masturbation – but stick with it. You are going to personalise the script that follows, then you are going to record yourself reading out the script. After that, you are going to listen to yourself and follow your own instructions – and it really works. It's not meant for anyone else; it's personal to you. So of course it's going to work.

An early twentieth-century advert for hypnotism in India. We can only imagine what these lessons would have been like and why there is the strange imagery at the top of the page. But ultimately, like this man, I am a fan of everybody learning hypnotism for themselves. It's the central theme of this book. The hypnotist has no special powers. That's right: we are all powerful.

Personal Lessons.

ARE you desirous of learning Hypnotism, Magnetic-Healing, Personal Magnetism, Graphology or Magic? Wouldn't you like to master any one or all of the above arts and become a stage Demonstrator? I will teach you practically. I can get you all the apparatus, Magical or otherwise used by the leading Magicians and Demonstrators of the world. In three days' time I can make you a practical hypnotist. You will be more than pleased with the results. I have taught Hypnotism to men in every walk of life for the last 8 years in Burma. Let me teach you too. If I could see you and speak to you, face to face, I am sure I can convince you in everything that I say. You may get the best books on the subject in this world but still you do require a master to give you practical lessons. You can have my personal lessons in your own home if you so desire it. Whether you are of my sex or the opposite sex you can learn Hypnotism. I have taught Hypnotism to many ladies who turned out good hypnotists and character readers. All dealings with me are strictly confidential. For fees and other particulars apply, (enclosing stamp) to—

The Stage Hypnotist
C/o Clarence Brothers
Silverdale
Upper Burma.   KANBALU.

If you have a specific problem, it's easy to see where to adapt the script. If not, simply insert the intention to feel confident, happy and full of energy and wellbeing. If there are any notions that you don't like, for example you don't like the idea of being in a forest because you find that scary, then make it a beach. This is yours, so make it what you like.

The internet is full of sample scripts that you can download and adapt for yourself. Once you've tried this one, you can really get into some detailed work on yourself. You can tackle weight loss, phobias, fatigue. Anything a standard hypnotherapist can do, you can do for yourself. It's about regular use. Listen to the whole recording whenever you have a moment, but you can also do a short remix version in your own head, whenever you need a few minutes to touch back in to yourself. I'm sure there's a lot of self-hypnosis going on in lavatory cubicles in offices all over the world right at this moment. I'm just too well brought-up to think about it.

It's worth a word at this point about expectation. These results will be subtle, quiet and absolutely profound. Don't expect the earth to shake, or for you to look different when you next look in the mirror, but do expect your habits to be more fluid, more plastic, less automatic.

It might take you a while to get used to the sound of your own voice. It's shocking how little we are exposed to this even now, surrounded as we are with recording technology. But give yourself the invitation to experience liking yourself through liking the sound of your own voice, and you'll be well on the way to a positive frame of mind. Why wouldn't you like the sound of your own voice anyway? It's the voice of the hypnotist. The one who is going to help you help yourself to heal.

Self-Hypnosis Script

Hello [name]. I am the hypnotist. You and I both know that I am you. That is
true. But it's also true to say that I am the hypnotist. I am going to help you.
I want you to sit or lie down, and get comfortable. We both know that it takes
you a while to get settled, so I'll give you time.

Now take a deep breath in. Breathe in slowly. There is no hurry. And exhale.
Deep slow, easy breaths.

Now, with your eyes open and turned slightly upwards, stare at something
in front of you.

Notice what you see, the colours and the light. [pause]

Now observe what you hear – the tempo, the volume and the character
of the sound. [pause]

Now observe what you feel – the temperature, the texture of your clothes,
gravity pulling you down towards earth, your breathing. [pause]

Notice what you see. [pause] Notice what you hear. [pause]
Now notice what you feel.

[name], I invite you to notice how heavy your eyelids are feeling. They are
growing heavier and heavier. How would it be if you allowed them to close?

Now turn your attention to the muscles in your head. The muscles in your
brow and the muscles around your eyes are getting soft, releasing. You feel
your cheeks getting softer. You feel the muscles in your lips relaxing, releasing.
Simply allowing any tension in the muscles of your face or in the top of your
head to release, I invite you to let go. Relaxing your neck, allowing the tension
to release, relax your shoulders and let them drop.

As your shoulders relax, your arms drop. Relax your upper arms, your lower
arms, your hands.

Relax each and every finger. Allow the muscles of your stomach to relax, and
your lower back.

Relax your hips, your buttocks. Relax your thighs, your calves, and shins. Relax
your feet and your toes. Now scan your body to see if there is any tension left,
and, if there is, just breathe into that tightness and let it go.

From your head to your toes, you have allowed yourself to become completely and totally relaxed.

As you count back from ten down to one you will relax more and more with each lower number.

10, 9, drifting deeper and deeper

8, 7, feeling a hundred times more relaxed

6, 5, 4, feeling a thousand times more relaxed

3, 2,

and now completely relaxed on 1.

Now imagine yourself in a place where you feel safe and serene, at ease and at home. This might be a real place or somewhere you are imagining. Just let the image come to you through any of your senses and when you're ready, begin to explore your place. How does it feel – is it warm or cold, what kind of smells are there, what colours are there, what does it sound like? Immerse yourself here. This is a wonderful private place, where only the best things can be. The best of you. Enjoy it. Take it all in, remember all the details.

Now walk around your place and find the spot where you feel even more at peace, even more connected. This is a magical place – where you draw from the deep sense of peacefulness you feel there. Take pleasure in the feeling of healing and rest.

This is the place where you can make the changes you want to make. Everything is possible here. This is the place to bring the things you are worried about and the place to imagine how easy it is to become the person who doesn't have a problem.

So, [name], I want you to think about [your worry, or problem]. I want you to think about a situation that has happened where this problem worried you. Really visualise this scene, and place yourself in the middle of the scene. When you played with that creatively, I want you to take a deep breath and enjoy the relaxation that is flowing through your body.

Now I'm going to invite you to experience that scene again, but this time bring all the calm, relaxed energy of your subconscious mind that you are feeling right now into your experience of the scene. This will make you more confident, calm and relaxed. When you are ready, replay the scene and see how different it is this time.

Wonderful. You are really good at this. Relax again and have a rest in the amazingly powerful feeling of confident relaxation you are feeling. So now, I'm going to invite you to repeat this process. In your own time, put yourself back in the scene that once you found difficult but now you find pleasant and easy.

And relax once more. Reflect on your experience of how easy your subconscious is playing creatively with these ideas. Take confidence from that. As I invite you for the last time to put yourself in that scene.

So now, I'm going to invite you to take three deep breaths. Really fill up your lungs and enjoy that feeling of change that each breath gives you. It is impossible for life to be exactly the same as it used to be after each of those breaths.

In a minute you are going to leave your healing place, knowing that you will come back as often as you need to energise and heal. You leave with a light heart knowing that you have changed your story.

So now. Counting from one to five, I am going to return you to full conscious awakening.

1. Coming back slowly, with each suggestion I have made, growing golden inside you
2. You begin to get in touch with your body once more
3. Allowing your muscles to move
4. Knowing success is assured you are happy to return fully to life on ...
5. Now why don't we be happy?

A HYPNOTIZED TEA PARTY.

THE DODGY STUFF

I'm a big hippy about hypnosis, aren't I? I love its possibilities; its potential to bring about change in what might feel like a stuck situation. I love its theatricality and hopefulness. But I have to admit that I also like the bad-boy bits of hypnosis too. I don't approve, naturally, but here are a handful of favourite moments from the wrong side of the hypnotic tracks.

Carl Sextus

Let's start gently. A favourite HypnoClassic is an American book by Carl Sextus called *Hypnotism: A Correct Guide to the Science and How Subjects are Influenced*. He gets full marks from me for claiming that mesmerism really ought to have been called Puysegurian Somnambulism. However he seems to have been most interested in hypnotic curiosities, which verge on odd and sometime career fatally into a world of wrong. For evidence of this, see the hypnotised lobster below.

Opposite: We have come across hypnotised tea parties before in these pages, but this is a beautiful illustration of just how much fun it could be. The man is Sextus himself, and the ladies are all cataleptic – 'motionless as statues' – which must have been terribly annoying, as the tea would go cold.

Below left: Sextus reports in detail about hypnotic stage shows that he has seen all over America in the last decades of the nineteenth century. This routine is fascinating because of what it reveals about US society. Of course a 'coloured' man would want to wash off his blackness.

HYPNOTIZED LOBSTER—CATALEPTIC STATE.

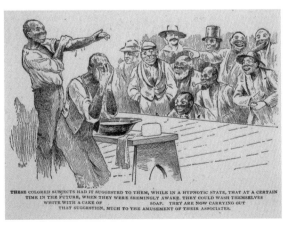

THESE COLORED SUBJECTS HAD IT SUGGESTED TO THEM, WHILE IN A HYPNOTIC STATE, THAT AT A CERTAIN TIME IN THE FUTURE, WHEN THEY WERE SEEMINGLY AWAKE, THEY COULD WASH THEMSELVES WHITE WITH A CAKE OF SOAP. THEY ARE NOW CARRYING OUT THAT SUGGESTION, MUCH TO THE AMUSEMENT OF THEIR ASSOCIATES.

There is nothing at all troublesome about this image, obviously. A priest hypnotising a tableful of boys and laying them all out prone... I'm sure it was all totally above board.

Stripnosis and Other Saucy Delights

You know when you stumble across something and it's really interesting, but it's a Pandora's Box. You want to tell people about it, but you know that when you tell them they won't be able to unknow it. Well I'm going to just say the words, and if you search for it on the internet then it's up to you. I've thought about it and decided that from everything I know about you, you're grown up enough. I'm talking about erotic hypnosis.

It had never occurred to me that there would be such a thing. But of course there is. Erotic stage hypnotists, erotic therapists who promise the best orgasm you have ever had without ever touching you. Lots and lots of people who just seem to want to be told what to do. I love the social

construct of this. You can have the kind of sex we might fantasise about, but only if you can tell yourself you were hypnotised. Being a sexual slave, being humiliated, having sex with a different gender than you are used to. It's all absolutely possible if you have the narrative that you were acting against your will. But as the items collected in these pages have repeatedly shown us, you can't be made to act against your will. Isn't it true that what we really fear is not what others might make us do, but what we secretly want to do? I say go for a walk on the wild side any time you want, but hypnosis is just an excuse. How would it be if you didn't need the excuse?

In our culture power is embedded deep in sexuality. The abuse of power and the pleasure that can be derived from it is all connected to the fact that women have

The use of hypnosis as a teaching aid in schools has long been overlooked. Here is an experiment from the 1950s.

The 10-month-old Persian cat owned by Arthur Newman of Jersey City, N.J., 13 March 1945. This isn't really dodgy as such – only if you think the cat is really hypnotising the lady. Staring at the cat is like looking at a fixed point on the ceiling, or at a bright light, or at a fob watch. It just makes the eyes tired and helps induce relaxation. It's a great image though, isn't it?

Oh crikey. Look at these evil gypsies and their devious hypnotic nastiness, being practised on a very Middle England chap. This is exactly what every decent person fears. I'd suggest that he will dream of this woman holding his hand at quiet moments of intense reflection for years to come, and it will turn out to be well worth the extra large note. But I don't condone crime, obviously.

had to be kept in their place by men, by any means necessary – from violence, to social and economic control. Hypnosis seems benign by comparison. But this is not the place to deconstruct the patriarchy, kids – let's talk hypnotic films instead …

To save you the bother of watching them, I'm going to reference three classic soft porn examples from the late 1960s and early 1970s. These are exploitation films of the highest order, but they have a certain kitsch appeal. Everything is summed up in *She Did What He Wanted* (1971) in which a man gets loads of women to do what he wants using hypnosis. He manages to get a whole stable of sex slaves, and all

for the outlay of a small pamphlet on how to hypnotise. The concept is reversed in *The Sadistic Hypnotist* from 1969, in which Wanda entraps masochistic men into doing what they really (don't) want to do. But the best title from the late 60s – if not the best plot – has to be *Stripnotised* (n.d) … a branch of hypnosis that really should live on in punland, if not in reality.

I like the joke, but there are many things online that really aren't funny in the least. There are websites offering to teach men how to seduce women using only hypnosis, promising that they will then become willing sex slaves. One site offers hypnotic poems that will have women going weak at the knees and pliant in the bedroom (allegedly). The banner headline is 'How ready are you to create some real Hypno Lust – and get women to do exactly what you want?'

Then there is a whole sub-genre of gay porn, which is a lovely thesis for someone to get their teeth into, in which the plot generally goes 'Oh dear, somebody has forced me to do something that my moral framework finds challenging but my libido quite fancies doing – but I was hypnotised, innit?''

Below left: I prefer this view of the use of mesmerism in warfare. How would it be if we got rid of weapons and just fought out issues using hypnotic powers?

Below right: *Life* magazine in 1942 photographed members of the military being put under hypnosis during a radio show. Presumably this wasn't part of a covert mission, but it might explain why the USA was so late entering World War II. Hypnosis on the wireless doesn't have a long and glorious history. Producers tend to be wary – I can't imagine why.

The Military

This is not the place to get into the Hitler as hypnotist issue. Even if he did employ some of the techniques, I don't think it was the most pressing or worrisome issue about him. But there have been rumours, conspiracy theories and research about the use of hypnosis in warfare since at least Helen of Troy.

ROBINSON IMAGINES AMERICA IN THE FIELD: IV.—A MESMERIC BARRAGE CRUMPLING UP AN ENEMY ATTACK.

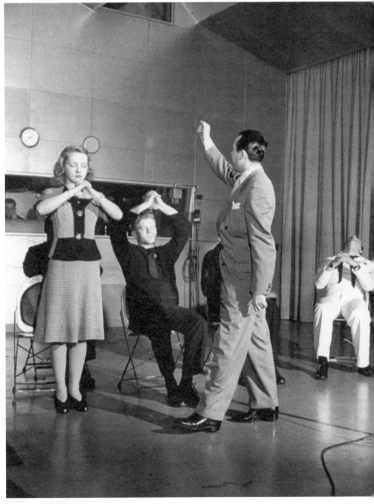

PAST LIFE REGRESSION

We've been taking a walk on the wild side of hypnosis, and firmly in this camp is past life regression. It is not hypnosis, but it uses it to recover what its proponents believe are memories of previous lives. It's done either for spiritual or therapeutic reasons, and is largely framed around not repeating past mistakes and letting go of the pain of previous lives.

The Art of Hypnotism by Joan Brandon. Our hypnotic heroine Joan Brandon attempts to cash in on the Bridey Murphy craze.

It's important to note that though there are various belief systems in human society that have reincarnation as central to their view of existence, mostly they don't teach that you can remember those lives or use a technique to access them. So past life regression that is all about remembering what you did in previous lives is definitely out on a limb. I have strong opinions on it, which I'm yearning to share, but I'm going to stay factual for as long as I can stand.

It has a rich cultural history. There is an ancient practice still around in yoga circles today called Prati Prasav, which involves releasing yourself from the mistakes and pain of past lives. But it was the brilliant Madame Blavatsky, Queen of the New Agers and founder of the Theosophical Society in the Victorian period, who brought the notion to the

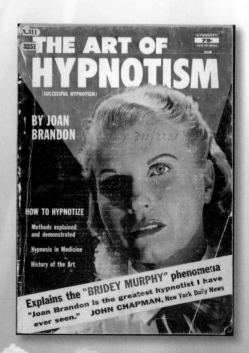

X.311

3251

A FAWCETT 75¢ HOW TO BOOK 308

THE ART OF HYPNOTISM

(SUCCESSFUL HYPNOTISM)

BY JOAN BRANDON

HOW TO HYPNOTIZE

Methods explained and demonstrated

Hypnosis in Medicine

History of the Art

Explains the "BRIDEY MURPHY" phenomena

"Joan Brandon is the greatest hypnotist I have ever seen." JOHN CHAPMAN, New York Daily News

Virginia Tighe, the
real-life Bridey Murphy,
chats with a neighbour
– probably discussing
why they live in a
maximum-security
facility built for toddlers.

modern world. Many of the tropes of
past life regression, such as mysterious
and sinister practitioners, and people
uncovering the notion that they were the
lady-in-waiting of Elizabeth I – come from
her descriptions. But the real heyday of
past life regression came in America in
the 1950s. An amateur hypnotist put a
housewife into a trance and wrote a book
about it. Virginia Tighe 'discovered' that she
had been Bridey Murphy – a dirt-poor
Irish girl from the nineteenth century.
What's so amazing, when reading about
the story, is not that it was eventually
debunked, but that it took such a hold
on the world. There were movies made
about the case, pop songs, reincarnation
parties and cocktails named after her.
Was America in the 1950s really so
affluent that they could spend valuable
time focusing on such things and

wondering if they were all true? By the
way, the movie – *The Search for Bridey
Murphy* (1956) – is a great watch. You can
find it for free online, and you can see why
people who know nothing about past life
regression think it's familiar. Films like this
have become part of our folk memory.
You might be aware of *The Devil Rides Out*
(1968), *On A Clear Day You Can See Forever*
(1970) and *Dead Again* (1991). It's a great
premise for a screenplay.

There is a vast amount of literature
and scientific studies on the subject of
past life regression, but I'm going to stride
past all of it and go headlong into my
personal experience. When I was studying
hypnotherapy we were warned to steer
clear of such things. We were told it was
the kind of practice that brought hypnosis
into disrepute: it was a lot of self-help
nonsense.

But I read *A Practical Guide to Past Life
Regression* by Florence Wagner McClain
(Llewellyn's New Age Series) at the British
Library and I realised that actually I had
all the skills I needed to regress people if I
wanted to. The question was, did I want to?
Well, first I thought I'd like to experience
it for myself. (The closest I'd ever got to it

was a lovely man I loved for a week who told me that he had been sent to a past life regression expert by his father. He had told his father he was a homosexual, and his father had obviously replied, 'You'd better have past life regression in case you weren't a lesbian in a former life who was raped by a solider.' This all seemed so

Llewellyn's New Age Series

A PRACTICAL GUIDE TO

PAST LIFE REGRESSION

"What we did yesterday shaped today. What we do today shapes tomorrow."

87 06060 Florence Wagner McClain

bonkers that I couldn't begin to unpack it.) So in the spirit of research, I booked an appointment to see a very nice lady. She used a really great technique that I'd like to share with you. It might sound like charlatanism, but I think it's really exciting in terms of freeing ourselves from our old narratives of what is true and what isn't. You don't have to believe it all, but it's a good game to play.

She asked many questions, and most of my answers were 'I don't know.' Things like 'Have you had previous lives?', 'Are any of your birthmarks from previous lives?', 'Is there anyone in your life now that you knew in previous lives?' You might answer 'no' straightaway, but I like to think of myself as open-minded and replied 'I don't know.' She would then say 'And if you did know?' I found myself starting to say 'yes' to some things and 'no' to others. I found that I had strong instincts either way, when before I would have said that I was highly sceptical about it all. So things started to get interesting, and engaging. After being put into hypnosis, I was instructed to walk down a corridor back to the time of my birth and beyond, and then to keep walking back until I had a strong sensation of something. Well I did, and it was very strong. I was in a smock and I was running through a field and I was undoubtedly a child. What followed was an incredibly exciting hour or so of going from past life to past life. About six in all. Most were fascinating, and some were awful and I felt tragic. It was so intense, and so stimulating. Do I think any of them were my previous lives? No way. I think it was a fantastic creative experience, led by a confident practitioner. I like stories; I'm a character comedian. I make up personalities for a living. Each of them has aspects of myself in them. Doing what I do creatively has a therapeutic aspect to it, and I think this was a speed-version of that. I left feeling really great about myself. The tears had come up because of things I had to resolve in my life, the joys because I'm a big fan of living and being playful. I recommend it wholeheartedly. Don't believe it, though.

It's interesting because one of my hypnotic heroes, Nicholas Spanos, who was a big fan of highlighting the role-playing factor in hypnosis, did lots of research into past life regression in the 1990s. I read his findings after I had been regressed. He basically concluded that people didn't

After being put into hypnosis, I was instructed to walk down a corridor back to the time of my birth and beyond, and then to keep walking back until I had a strong sensation of something. Well I did, and it was very strong. I was in a smock and I was running through a field and I was undoubtedly a child.

get in touch with memories from other lives, but were influenced by all the inputs around them – from literature, film, TV and childhood stories – mixed with a huge part of the subject's own life, all mashed up with the expectations of the practitioner. This is especially true in highly hypnotisable subjects, and this completely chimes with my experience. I say, try it for yourself. It's cheaper than a day spa and much more fun.

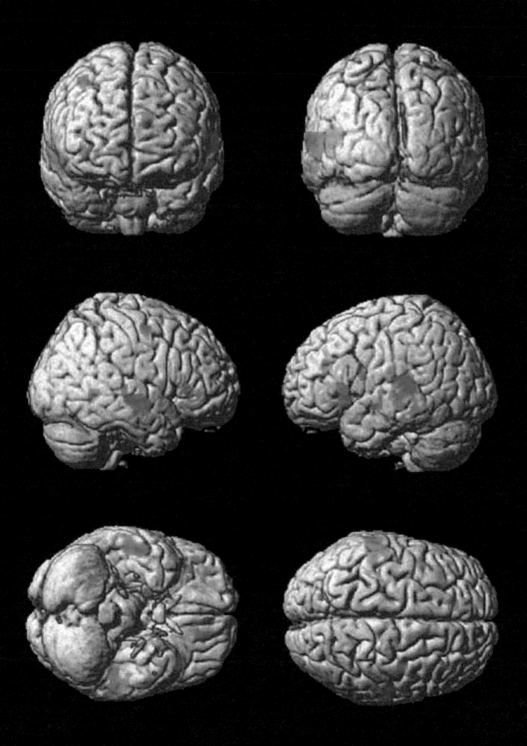

THE NEURO-SCIENCE

Oh Lord, I love a brain scan. Not having one, obviously, because that would be weird. No, I like looking at them. Sort of pretending to understand exactly what they're showing me. They are strangely satisfying – and the best thing is that they kind of make sense experientially.

If you see an image of an ordinary person scanned in the middle of a busy day alongside the brain of a Buddhist monk who meditates for eight hours daily, the jumble of lit-up areas in the ordinary person's brain will look like your head feels. You yearn for what appears to be the tranquillity going on in the monk's brain. If you were to swap the captions I'm not 100 per cent sure I could tell the difference, but it's like catnip. I'm hooked.

I'm not unusual, of course. Witness the fact that so many documentaries and vaguely medical articles will give you a saucy flash of a brain scan, to back up any hypothesis being made. The more popular papers show us what our brains look like when we're in love, and guess what – in the middle of our brain is pink neon in the shape of a heart. Of course there is! We knew it all along.

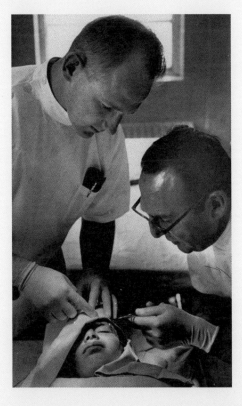

Ohhh – this is what you might imagine neurohypnotists to look like. White coats, a bit sinister. It's totally misleading. Sorry. This is actually an image of 1950s American surgeons using hypnosis as an anaesthetic while stitching up a boy's eye.

Brain areas activated during actual pain (left column), hypnotivcally suggested pain (centre) and imagined pain (right). The top five images in each column are brain scans and the bottom two show the same activity superimposed on left and right sides of a standard brain.

So, because I want to give you what you didn't realise you wanted until just now, we're going to look at the very modern relationship between neuroscience and hypnosis, and I'm going to give you some scan-porn in the shape of MRI images of the brain during hypnosis.

Psychologists and neuroscientists have been scanning the brains of hypnotised people recently as a way of potentially revealing how the brain normally works, in the hope that it will explain medically baffling neurological disorders. Unlike the other sections of this book, this is not really about hypnosis for its own sake, it's about what hypnosis reveals about our brains functioning well, or functioning badly. For that reason it's probably the most important section — even if, disappointingly, there aren't any instructions on how to hypnotise a lobster, or images of anyone slumped over a chaise longue. But it's important because anything that a hypnotic practitioner can do to a subject, the subject can do to themselves using self-hypnosis and with a little training. This is very exciting. Self-hypnosis — or whatever name it comes to be called in the future — could well be just the tool we need to deal

with the joyful burden of consciousness. In the spirit of reliance on yourself rather than medical professionals, this mechanism — once it's stripped of the whiff of both showbiz and hippy bollocks — could really help the human race to face up to the awesomely frightening challenge of having a brain and being alive. So far this battle is being lost in a morass of addiction, depression and self-loathing as the twenty-first century progresses, so we need all the strategies we can get.

I'm about as far from a neuroscientist as it's possible to be, so don't zone out — if I can get my head around, it then you all can. We're going to look at just two ideas from this area. (An area I doubt you will want to think of as neurohypnosis.) The point of this might seem obscure, but I reckon it's really important: it shows how little we understand about what is going on in hypnosis. 'Well, so what?' you might ask (if you're in the habit of talking to the book you are reading).

Well, what we call hypnosis now has been going on in our brains since we were first human, and it will carry on until there *are* no more humans. At this stage of our cultural development we happen to call it hypnosis. It also happens to be regarded by the vast majority of human beings as something of a joke, by many others as irrelevant, and even those of us who are fascinated by it tend to focus more on the big moustaches and kitchsy, campy, quirky notions of the big-mouthed practitioners of the subject. But it belongs to all of us. It's a human process. What exactly is going on chemically, biochemically and bioelectrically isn't known, but we are fools if we think it's just the preserve of men in spandex shirts. It's the people in the white coats that we should be interested in, especially in our age of increasing mental dis-ease. These days, it's much more acceptable to alter your brain chemistry using powerful drugs in the hope that a tiny percentage of its efficacy will help with lifting your mood. And yet, harnessing what is after all a perfectly natural human process – one person simply helping another to experience something – is thought of as a bit sinister and weird. So I salute the neurohypnotism research. I suspect that in a few hundred years, when some irreverent and light-hearted comedian writes a round-up of their thinking on hypnosis using books from

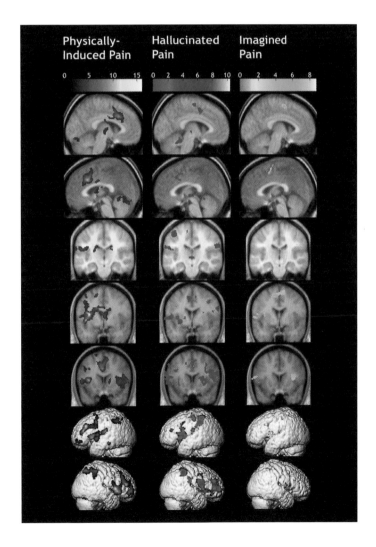

Top: brain regions that **decrease** in activation with increasing depth of hypnosis. Bottom: brain regions that **increase** in activation with increasing depth of hypnosis.

our time, they will look at this one and say 'Christopher was over-focused on typeface, bill matter and moustaches, but he was right about the neuroscience. It was after all what they called hypnosis back then, that proved the turning point in helping human beings fight back from the damaging mental ill-health caused by fighting the squishing effects of capitalism on a daily basis.' (I can dream, can't I?)

But enough of being a neurohypnotic Martin Luther King … all I'm doing is proving how much unlike a scientist I am – all vision and no factual basis. But I'm trying.

So here is something that is clear to understand. We all know about pain,

right? Oh sister, oh brother, we all know about pain! But how is pain manifested in the brain? And can it be faked? (Brace yourselves for a brain scan.)

So what you can see here are the areas of the brain that are stimulated when someone is in actual pain. That's the part on the left. Several areas light up, brighter than a Beyoncé-audience blind-light (you know what a blind-light is – where lights from the back of the stage shine on the audience for a couple of seconds, just before the beat kicks in, and a temporarily invisible Beyoncé blows her nose on the floor). Second from right is when the person is asked to imagine being in pain. Hardly anything happens. It's like the lighting at a particularly dull folk music gig. We creatively play with the idea of being in pain enough so that we can recall what it might be like, but not enough to trouble the physical workings of our brains. But second from left is what happens when the experience of pain is suggested in hypnosis. The same areas as those that are active when we are actually in pain light up – but just not to the same extent. This is like a Solange Knowles gig rather than a Beyoncé show, but still way,

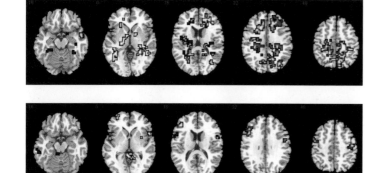

> **All those nineteenth-century images of small fellas or weak-willed women being 'put under' by high-status hypnotists belie what was really going on. The brains of the subjects were fizzing with activity, probably way more than the brain of the hypnotist, who was doing what he did hundreds of times a day.**

way more than the folk gig. Nobody is really sure why hypnosis provokes such a strong reaction but – do you get my point? – you would be a fool to ignore the effectiveness that this scan reveals. We need to keep researching it. Our brains are (ironically) more powerful than we have the brain power to even contemplate, and how do we spend our lives? Waiting for computers to boot up, download and buffer themselves, while doping ourselves on prescription antidepressants or self-medicating with alcohol or other legal or illegal drugs. Wake up and let's celebrate our own brain power, my friends. As Professor Harradan termed it – 'mysterious science' indeed!

Some of the most interesting work is around what's called the default mode network. I like this because, again, it's quite experiential – you can sort of feel it happening in your own head. This is the part of the brain that is active when you are at wakeful rest. It uses up a huge amount of energy, so there must be something going on. The DMN takes over when you are doing jobs that demand just a bit of attention, and has been linked to daydreaming, episodic memory

lapses and general self-awareness. Being 'miles away'. When subjects were hypnotised, however, they showed much less activity in the DMN and more activity in the prefrontal attentional systems. In other words, though being relaxed and hypnotised might look like resting and drifting off, like when you're doing the washing up, in fact the brain is way more active during hypnosis. It's a very busy state. The brain is highly engaged, responding to those suggestions, actively playing with them. This tells us a lot about how our brains function most of the time when we are not hyper-engaged, and makes us think differently about what is going on while a subject is hypnotised.

All those nineteenth-century images of small fellas or weak-willed women being 'put under' by high-status hypnotists belie what was really going on. The brains of the subjects were fizzing with activity, probably way more than the brain of the hypnotist, who was doing what he did hundreds of times a day. Most likely he was focusing on whether the photographer was making him look chubby in his waistcoat or whether he had combed his moustache enough. I like this revisionary view of history.

Crucially, it also tells us about our brains under ordinary modern conditions. When mechanically browsing Facebook or Twitter, or scrolling through shopping options online, or even endless over-the-top pornographic images, we go into a trance state – but this trance is much more like the dulled state when the DMN kicks in than a trance associated with hypnosis. It's got a lot more in common with peeling potatoes than being hypnotised. It takes much more energy to meditate or self-hypotise than it does to scroll through brightly-coloured lists on a smartphone. Never before have human beings needed mindful practices like this to stop the descent into mass semi-somnambulism. So beware of that dangerous Dr Caligari in your pocket. That's the modern-day expressionist horror story.

It takes much more energy to meditate or self-hypotise than it does to scroll through brightly-coloured lists on a smartphone. Never before have human beings needed mindful practices like this to stop the descent into mass semi-somnambulism.

I mentioned that this stuff might only be taken seriously once we move on from the word 'hypnosis'. It needs serious rebranding. I think that's a shame, because as you can see from this book, I celebrate all the bright shouts and all the dark shameful whispers in the history of the hypnosis, but to the average person it's just too confusing. Could it be time to change the name? A contemporary hypnotic hero is Dr Amir Raz. He started off as a magician while studying to be a doctor. He says 'Magic taught me a lot about psychology in terms of attention, directing attention and how the mind works. At one point I started reading about hypnosis and decided to marry the two.' However, he acknowledges the need for the rebrand and I like his solution, although for me it's a bit worthy and not spunky enough.

'Hypnosis is tricky because it has such a checkered history. Many people feel uncomfortable with it, even within the scientific community, because they think it's not something that a serious scientist should get involved in. Part of the reason it has this bad reputation is because of things like stage hypnosis, where you see a bunch of people clucking like chickens.'

Dr Raz therefore suggests ditching 'hypnosis' in favour of 'focused attention' or 'susceptibility to suggestion'.

This is not a million miles away from the term coined by James Coates in 1905, 'suggestive therapeutics', though as I've pointed out, this is likely to get people in cahoots with pimps rather than psychiatrists. But though his new names don't zing, Dr Raz makes a rallying cry for the future of the subject. 'I don't consider myself a hypnosis researcher. If anything, I'm more of a neuroscientist with an interest in attention. I see hypnosis as an interesting tool for illuminating interesting scientific questions about consciousness, volitional control and authorship.'

Of course, I want to challenge myself and think of a new term for hypnosis that takes all of the history and all the modern neuroscience into account. I want to be a twenty-first-century rebranding Braid. But then he cocked up with the name hypnosis, introducing all sorts of notions of sleep and so on that have misled people ever since. I'm sure I'll do the same. But I'll have a go. Please contact me with your own suggestions and let's solve this one ...

Here are mine:
Suggestnosis
Relaxed wakefulness
Suggest-ability
Attention therapy
Green power (following in the footsteps of Walford Bodie and the Bodic Force)
Oh dear. Your turn!

MY STORY

PART FOUR

've charted my journey from knowing nothing about hypnosis to it being a big part of my life. I think it's only fair to let you know how the love story ends. As is so often the case, it ends with one of the pair leaving the other behind. Not entirely, you understand; we still meet regularly for coffee for old times' sake. But yes, dear reader, I'm sorry to say that hypnosis and I are no longer exclusive with each other.

It was hypnosis that first suggested to me that I could have a different relationship with my thoughts; that I could relate differently to my self-narrative. This is so incredibly powerful. It also revealed to me that profound change is incredibly subtle – so that the difference between delight and despair is not black and white, but one of 50 million shades of grey. You can be happy or unhappy in every situation, because every situation contains both possibilities. Love and loss are the same thing. It's not loss if you never loved, and it's not love if it doesn't contain the possibility of the agony of loss. These things are so subtle and so rich. It's only a slight exaggeration to say that I used to think it was simple: you shouted when you were happy and you cried when you were sad. The thought that you could be feeling both and yet you

just smile and keep on walking to the post office hadn't occurred to me.

The big change that happened was witnessing the illness and death of the person who was closest to me in the world. Something like that either pushes you into profound change or profound pain. So I don't credit hypnosis with the whole thing. It was the framework I was studying at the time, but it is big enough and flexible enough to cope with that, as well as casual and flippant enquiry.

I used self-hypnosis every day during this terrible time of my life when my husband was dying. I would walk on the beach and go into a state that was far removed from the possibility of loss and was pure play and escape. By being totally present with the wind and the waves and the sand I was totally present with my feelings. I wasn't avoiding anything; I was touching in to the essential things about me that being in pain couldn't touch. It was this playfulness that helped me see a version – or multiple versions – of myself afterwards.

One of the last modules we studied on the hypnotherapy course was on mindfulness, or being fully in the moment – turning towards pain or difficulty. It was extraordinary for me in that classroom, because many of the principles of the practice I had worked out for myself. I had my own words for concepts outlined in mindfulness class. It was like hearing a private language you thought only you knew being spoken in public. Of course I had to find out more, and I studied with a teacher and then learned to be a teacher of it myself. I started a daily mediation practice that I can't imagine ever being without now. I also remember some of the early formal mediation sessions: I would literally shout at myself. I couldn't believe how loud my brain was; how noisy and chattery my thoughts were. I would start to shake and be furious with myself. Then I gradually realised that this had been going on for years and I'd never noticed – never paid it any attention. All of that self-judgement, self-narrative and self-abuse. A lot of it was at heart motivated by self-care, but self-care manifesting as pure worry. I try to have positive self-care now. If this all sounds like utter bollocks to you, just take the message that I try to be nice to myself. All right?

If you don't know much about mindfulness I urge you to go and find out more. It was first outlined as a way to deal with chronic pain by the Pain Research Unit at the University of Massachusetts. Instead of taking away the pain, patients were encouraged to sit with their pain and ask themselves if they could stand it in that moment. Its meditative and contemplative aspects came from Buddhism, with the spirituality stripped out; a bold, pragmatic move. Because as soon as someone like me hears that, they are going to want to find out what happens when you

That's why hypnosis as we understand it today has been around a long time, in entertainment venues and in consulting rooms. Because it's not something that's done to us by dodgy blokes with bow ties. It is us.

strip the spirituality back in. So, more
nervous than when I took myself off to
study stage hypnotism with the hypnotic
branch of UKIP, I started to go to Buddhist
meditation retreats. What I found there
and found within myself is not what this
book is about. But I wouldn't be here
without hypnosis. So every time I say to
someone on stage 'Listen to the sound
of my voice,' I do not say it lightly. I know
from my own life that I have had great
comfort, great provocation, great challenge
and great benefit from hypnosis. When
I ask punters to entertain the notion that
they can hold two contradictory truths in
their heads at the same time – usually in
relation to clasping their hands together
and being unable to pull them apart – I
can say that because I know since my
husband's death that I am totally fine and
totally fucked. Both are true. I may wear
a flashy suit, and sing big numbers, and
we may all dance together – but I do it
because this stuff goes deep. That's why
hypnosis as we understand it today has
been around a long time, in entertainment
venues and in consulting rooms. Because
it's not something that's done to us by
dodgy blokes with bow ties. It is us.

SUMMING UP

So, after all that, what is hypnosis?

If you want hard empirical facts, flick back through the previous chapters. Look at the names, look at the dates, look at the studies and the scientific data. All of that stuff is interesting and highly engaging, but we've spent enough time together now for you to suspect that that's not where my interest lies. I'm not going to argue to the death about state versus non-state, or which induction works better than another, or the minutiae of the ethics of hypnosis as entertainment. I said at the start of the book and at intervals throughout that, as in most other fields of human endeavour, there are many people who have a lot invested in making hypnosis incredibly complex. They will use big words, big data, big complicated machines even, to make hypnosis seem *other* than us. But I like it because, above all, it is experiential. It can only be experienced through experiencing it. I read an amazing piece recently as part of a play I'm making about pornography. It was about research into the mechanics of orgasm. At no point did it ever read like anyone involved in that project had ever had one. I know there has to be

objectivity and scholarly precision; I'm not criticising that aspect of it. I'm just worried that when something is argued, fought over, examined and quantified it risks becoming something removed from us. After all, all we have is our consciousness. All we have is our experience. There are many people highly invested in owning our orgasms. Similarly there are a lot of people interested in owning hypnosis – interested in them defining for you what it is and what is isn't.

I am not one of these people. I say, read the history, learn some techniques, and have cause to be thankful to those

---

Hypnosis is not about being Overpowered. Nobody can take control of you. In fact it's the exact opposite: hypnosis is a tool that you can use so that you are never Overpowered again – not by your fears, emotions or anxieties.

---

that have gone before and discovered things for us, saving us the bother. And then, experience it for yourself. I finished my story in the last chapter by saying that *hypnosis is us*. It is. Hypnosis is you.

Hypnosis is all the things in this book. The ones that mean the most to me are those that reflect the idea that it is 'as if'. Those that ask the question 'how would it be if …' It's the encouragement of a light state of playfulness that has the potential for deep impact. I hope you find the aspects of hypnosis that mean the most to you.

Hypnosis is not about being Overpowered. Nobody can take control of you. In fact it's the exact opposite: hypnosis is a tool that you can use so that you are never Overpowered again – not by your fears, emotions or anxieties.

Ultimately hypnosis is a flexible phenomenon that might be called something else in a few years' time. So, you know what, sweetheart? Don't worry about hypnosis. It's all things to all people. It's not fussy. It doesn't care. It's just your brain and the way it talks to itself. The induction spirals, the slick patter, the MRI scans, the self-help downloads, all turn out to be just manifestations of the way we relate to ourselves. And there's always the possibility that that relationship can improve. It could deepen, be more nurturing, more compassionate, more wonderful. It's that simple. It's that profound.

ILLUSTRATIONS

p. 49 'The Catateptic State', *The Magnetic and Botanic Family Physician* by D. Younger, 1887. British Library (7410.dh.53).

p. 51 (left) 'Making the Magnetic Pass, for Producing or Deepening the Mesmeric State', *The Magnetic and Botanic Family Physician* by D. Younger, 1887. British Library (7410.dh.53).

p. 51 (right) *The Practical Hypnotist* by James Coates, 1905. British Library (7410.ccc.22).

p. 52 *Secrets of Stage Hypnotism* by Karlyn (J. F. Burrows), 1912. British Library (7911.b.27).

p. 53 *Secrets of Stage Hypnotism* by Karlyn (J. F. Burrows), 1912. British Library (7911.b.27).

p. 56 Poster for Dr Zomb, Ormond McGill's stage act, 1960. Private collection.

p. 57 Pope Pius XII, 1945. AP/Press Association Images.

p. 59 Dave Elman raising subject's hand, c. 1951. Photograph courtesy Dave Elman Hypnosis Institute.

p. 62 *Life* magazine, 10 November 1941. British Library (P.P.6383.cke).

p. 63 *LSD, Marijuana, Yoga and Hypnosis* by Theodore X. Barber, 1971. British Library (YK.2009.a.10288).

p. 64 Early 20th-century mentalist or mind reader in costume. Vintage Images/Alamy.

p. 65 Poster for Handy Bandy and Nadia Nadyr, Hamburg, 1927. Interfoto/ Alamy.

pp. 66–67 *The Bodie Book* by Walford Bodie, 1905. British Library (7409.e.12).

p. 68 LP sleeve cover for *The Basic Principles of Kreskin's ESP*, released 1970. Private collection.

p. 69 Douglas Watson demonstrating a mass hypnotism at Enfield, 6 November 1951. Popperfoto/Getty Images.

p. 70 Poster advertising the appearance of Peter Casson at the Empire Theatre Leeds, 19 November 1956. Private collection.

p. 71 *Paul McKenna's Hypnotic Secrets*, 1995. British Library (YK.1996.b.10131).

p. 72 Psychotherapist Anatoly Kashpirovsky running a mass hypnosis séance, April 1988. RIA Novosti/Alamy.

p. 73 A woman dances on stage during a curative session conducted by psychotherapist Anatoly Kashpirovsky, July 1989. RIA Novosti/Alamy.

p. 74 Poster advertising Derren Brown's show, London, 2008. Hugh Sturrock/Alamy.

p. 75 Early 20th-century poster for Barnum Hypnotist. Library of Congress Prints and Photographs Division, Washington, D.C.

p. 76 Christopher Green. Courtesy the author.

p. 80 Original illustration by George du Maurier to *Trilby*, 1895. British Library (K.T.C.27.b.4).

p. 82 (left) 'Development of Mesmeric Science', cartoon by George du Maurier, *Punch Almanack* 1884. British Library (C.194.b.199).

p. 82 (right) Original illustration by George du Maurier to *Trilby*, 1895. British Library (K.T.C.27.b.4).

p. 83 *La Svengali Waltz* by Otto Roeder, 1895. Music to accompany the stage adaptation of Trilby. British Library (H.3667.a.13).

p. 85 Lobby card for *The Hypnotic Eye*, 1960. Private Collection.

p. 86 Woody Allen's *Broadway Danny Rose*, 1984. Photos 12/Alamy.

p. 87 *The Seven-Per-Cent Solution*, 1976. Photos 12/Alamy.

p. 88 *The Man Who Could Work Miracles*, 1936. Pictorial Press Ltd/ Alamy.

p. 90 *Svengali in Disguise* by Harry von Tilzer, 1902. National Museum of American History, Smithsonian Institution, Washington D.C.

p. 91 *How I Mesmerise 'Em* by Harry Castling, 1893. British Library (H.3980.h.(23)).

p. 92 *A full discovery of the strange practices of Dr Elliotson*, 1842. Wellcome Images.

p. 93 Mr Barham hypnotises his servant who manifests clairvoyance when in the hypnotic state, illustration to the short story *Barham's Servant* in *Cassell's Magazine*, 1891. British Library (P.P.6004.da).

p. 94 Woman being hypnotised, 1956. Carl Iwasaki/The LIFE Images Collection/Getty Images.

p. 95 Charcot demonstraing hysteria in a patient at the Salpêtrière, lithograph after P.A. Brouillet, 1887. Wellcome Images

p. 96 (left) Poster for 'Miss Annie de Montford Mesmeric Seances' at the Music Hall Barnstaple, 1881. British Library (Evanion 517).

p. 96 (right) Advertisement for Annie de Montford at the Music Hall Barnstaple, 1881. British Library (Evanion 1781).

p. 97 Poster for Annie de Montford at the Oxford Hall, Ilfracombe, 1881. British Library (Evanion 260).

p. 98 Poster for Mr and Mrs Herbert L. Flint, c. 1895. Library of Congress Prints and Photographs Division, Washington, D.C.

p. 99 Poster for Mrs Herbert L. Flint, 'the little hypnotic sunbeam', c. 1899. Library of Congress Prints and Photographs Division, Washington, D.C.

pp. 100–101 The Art of Hypnotism by Joan Brandon, 1956. British Library (X.311/3251).

p. 102 Christopher Green. Courtesy the author.

p. 104 Derek Diamond. Courtesy the author.

p. 107 Title page to Avicennae Canonis…, 1520. Wellcome Images.

p. 108 Henry Blythe gives his daughter Sally advice before she starts a driving lesson in Torquay, 15 January 1960. Anoymous/AP/Press Association Images.

p. 109 (above) Henry Blythe hypnotizes his daughter Sally at their home in Torquay, 15 January 1960, before taking her out for a driving lesson. AP/Press Association Images.

p. 109 (below) The Truth about Hypnotism by Henry Blythe, 1971. British Library (X.319/4322).

p. 110 Ralph Albert and son, Joe, look over some of the equipment he uses in hypnosis experiments, 30 March 1966. Jeff Goode/Toronto Star via Getty Images.

p. 111 Group of eight people under the influence of a rotary mirror apparatus (after Luys), Hypnotism and the New Witchcraft by E.A. Hart, 1893. British Library (7410.df.48).

p.112 (left) UK Patent GB191311392 – Improvments in or relating to Apparatus for Inducing Hypnotic Sleep. Inventors Hermani Emile Guilhaumon and Marcel Ferrand. 1913. Espacenet/European Patent Office.

p. 112 (right) UK Patent GB189916357 – An improved means for use in or connected with the cure of Insomnia. Inventor Allan Bennett MacGregor. 1899. Espacenet/European Patent Office.

p. 113 (left) UK Patent GB190925210 – Appliances for Inducing Sleep. Inventor: Haydn Brown. 1910. Espacenet/European Patent Office.

p. 113 (right) UK Patent GB233309 – Improved apparatus for inducing sleep. Inventors Hans Salomon and Max Friedrich. 1924. Espacenet/European Patent Office.

p. 114 US Patent US3822693 – Method for inducing hypnosis. Inventor P. King. 1974. United States Patent Office.

p. 115 (left) US Patent US20100168504 – Method and apparatus for the aid of meditation and hypnosis. 2010. United States Patent Office.

p. 115 (right) US Patent 6293874 – User-operated amusement apparatus for kicking the user's buttocks. Inventor Joe W. Armstrong. 2000. United States Patent Office.

p. 116 Harley Street Hypnotist by Alan Mitchell, 1960. British Library (012212.a.1/252).

p. 117 'A hard interview made easy', Personal Magnetism, Psychic Research Company, 1900. Mary Evans Picture Library/Alamy.

p. 118 The Illustrated Practical Mesmerist, Curative and Scientific by W. Davey, 1854. British Library (1404.b.4).

p. 119 Performing a caesarean under hypnosis. BSIP SA/Alamy.

p. 122 A record recorded by a hypnotist shall help healing. The enlarged photography of an eye zone is supposed to strengthen the effect of the works. Circa 1930. Imagno/Getty Images.

p. 126 Early 20th-century advert for a course in hypnotism in India. British Library (ORW.1986.a.5371).

p. 130 'A Hypnotised Tea Party', Hypnotism. Its facts, theories and related phenomena by Carl Sextus, 1896. British Library (7410.dh.20).

p. 131 (left) From Hypnotism. Its facts, theories and related phenomena by Carl Sextus, 1896. British Library (7410.dh.20).

p. 131 (right) A Hypnotised Lobster – cataleptic state, *Hypnotism. Its facts, theories and related phenomena* by Carl Sextus, 1896. British Library (7410.dh.20).

p. 132 Monk demonstrating lethargy techniques of hypnotism, 1959. Frank Scherschel/The LIFE Picture Collection/Getty Images.

p. 133 (top) Dr David Briggs' class in mental hygiene relaxes under hypnosis at Maryville Tennessee College, 1959. Everett Collection Historical/Alamy.

p. 133 (bottom) At a demonstration at the British Maritime Service Seamen's Institute in New York, 13 March 1945, Alma Davies succumbs to Puffy's hypnotic eyes while Newman holds the animal. AP/Press Association Images.

p. 134 When gypsies offer to read the hand of Signor F.Z. at Rho Milan, they hypnotise him and then rob him, illustration by Walter Molino in *La Domenica del Corriere*, 12 January 1958. Mary Evans Picture Library/Alamy.

p. 135 (left) 'A Mesmeric Barrage' by William Heath Robinson in *The Sketch*, 18 December 1918. British Library (HIU.LS52).

p. 135 (right) Military personnel being put under hypnosis during a radio program, 1943. Charles E. Steinheimer/The LIFE Picture Collection/Getty Images.

p. 136 *The Art of Hypnotism* by Joan Brandon. British Library (X.311/3251).

p. 137 Virginia Tighe, the real-life Bridey Murphy, chats with a neighbour, Mrs Russell Noll, over the back fence of her home, 11 October 1956. AP/Press Association Images.

p. 138 *A Practical Guide of Past Life Regression* by Florence Wagner McClan, 1986. British Library (87/06060).

p. 140 Brain under hypnosis. 3D MRI scans showing areas of activation (red) within a human brain when regions of the body move whilst under hypnosis. The specific areas that show activity here are: anterior cingulate cortex, parietal lobe, temporal lobe and cerebellum. Hubert Raguet/Look at Sciences/Science Photo Library.

p. 141 Hypnosis being used as an aid in medicine instead of anaesthetic while stitching up a boy's head would, 1958. Carl Mydans/The LIFE Picture Collection/Getty Images.

p. 143 Cerebral activation during hypnotically induced and imagined pain, *NeuroImage*, 23, 392–401, Derbyshire, S.W.G., Whalley, M.G., Stenger A.V. & Oakley D.A. (2004). Courtesy David Oakley.

p. 144 Modulating the default mode network using hypnosis. *International Journal of Clinical and Experimental Hypnosis* 60, 206–228, Deeley, Q., Oakley, D.A., Toone, B., Gampietro, V., Brammer, M.J., Williams, S.C.R. & Halligan, P.W. (2012). Courtesy David Oakley.

p. 148 Christopher Green. Courtesy the author.

p. 151 The Singing Hypnotist. Courtesy the author.

INDEX

For my son Archie.

Thank you to:
Professor David Oakley
Professor Christopher French
Anthony Jacquin and all at HeadHacking
    and ChangePhenomena
Max Kirsten
Donald Robertson
Jamie Andrews, Zoe Wilcox and Jon Fawcett
    and all the curators who helped at the
    British Library
Duncan Walsh-Atkins, Seiriol Davies, Jenny Carr
    and Michael Roulston for playing for
    the Singing Hypnotist
All the participants who have been part
    of the Singing Hypnotist
The Wellcome Trust for supporting the
    development of Overpowered and the
    Singing Hypnotist
The Leverhulme Trust for supporting my
    residency at the British Library
Abby Singer, Mel Keynon and all at
    Casarotto Ramsay
Special thanks to Jonah Albert

In memory of Ben Harmer (1971–2009)
"When I think that I'm over you,
I'm overpowered"

For more information on
The Singing Hypnotist visit
www.christophergreen.net

First published in 2015 by
The British Library
96 Euston Road
London NW1 2DB

Text copyright © Christopher Green 2015
Images copyright © The British Library Board
and other named copyright-holders 2015

Cataloguing in Publication Data
A catalogue record for this publication
is available from The British Library

ISBN 978 0 7123 5785 2

Designed by Briony Hartley, Goldust Design
Picture research by Sally Nicholls
Printed in Hong Kong by
Great Wall Printing Co. Ltd